CONSTABLE AMONG THE HEATHER

BY THE SAME AUTHOR

as Nicholas Rhea
Constable on the Hill
Constable on the Prowl
Constable Around the Village
Constable Across the Moors
Constable in the Dale
Constable by the Sea
Constable Along the Lane
Constable Through the Meadow
Constable in Disguise
Portrait of the North York Moors

as Peter N. Walker
Murders and Mysteries from the North York Moors
Folk Tales from the North York Moors
Carnaby and the Hijackers
Carnaby and the Gaolbreakers
Carnaby and the Assassins
Carnaby and the Conspirators
Carnaby and the Saboteurs
Fatal Accident
Panda One on Duty
Special Duty
Carnaby and the Eliminators
Identification Parade
Carnaby and the Demonstrators
Panda One Investigates
Carnaby and the Infiltrators
The Dovingsby Death
Carnaby and the Kidnappers
The MacIntyre Plot
Missing from Home
Witchcraft for Panda One
Target Criminal
Carnaby and the Counterfeiters
The Carlton Plot
Siege for Panda One
Teenage Cop
Carnaby and the Campaigners
Robber in a Mole Trap

as Christopher Coram
A Call to Danger
A Call to Die
Death in Ptarmigan Forest
Death on the Motorway
Murder by the Lake
Murder beneath the Trees
Prisoner on the Dam
Prisoner on the Run

as Tom Ferris
Espionage for a Lady

as Andrew Arncliffe
Murder after the Holiday

Constable Among the Heather

NICHOLAS RHEA

ROBERT HALE • LONDON

First published in Great Britain 1990

ISBN 0 7090 4140 3

Robert Hale Limited
Clerkenwell House
Clerkenwell Green
London EC1R 0HT

Set by Selectmove Ltd, London
Printed in Great Britain by St Edmundsbury Press,
Bury St Edmunds, Suffolk and
Bound by WBC Bookbinders

Contents

1 *Daffodil Duty*

In nature, there are neither rewards nor punishments – there are consequences.
Robert Green Ingersoll (1833–99)

High on the moors above Aidensfield there is a lonely farmstead. A farmer and his wife worked its upland fields all their married life; it was a tough, never-ending task with little monetary reward but they raised a family and saw their small heather-encircled property increase in value. When retirement beckoned, the couple sold their farm to settle in a cottage at Elsinby.

During their working life, they had never had a holiday, but twice a month or so the husband had enjoyed a day at the cattle mart, while occasionally his wife had gone shopping to York or joined a WI outing to Scarborough. So far as a longer holiday was concerned, neither had had any wish to go away and, besides, someone had to care for the livestock for twenty-four hours a day, 365 days a year.

As a retirement present, their children decided to send the couple overseas. They selected a trip to Switzerland which would include all the excitement of flying and the sheer joy of exploring a foreign country. On the first night, when their parents would be in their room, the children rang them at the hotel to see how they were coping.

From the discussion that followed, it was evident they were thoroughly enjoying themselves, and then their son asked, 'Dad, what's the view like from your bedroom window?'

'There isn't one,' said the old man. 'But there would be, if it wasn't for all these mountains.'

I mention this yarn because the people who live on the heights of the North York Moors are so accustomed to dramatic and long-distance views that vistas from other places are often disappointing. It is claimed that upon the moors you don't have to go seeking views; they offer themselves to be enjoyed. Such visitors as William Wordsworth and John Wesley have admired some of our views, modern tourists now come and attempt to identify distant towns and hills from the many vantage-points, and there is even a claim that the towers of Lincoln Cathedral can be seen from one particular place – and that cathedral stands over one hundred miles to the south. Certainly there are views which extend for fifty miles or so, and without doubt many are stunning in their range. Examples include the famous vista from Sutton Bank Top on the A170, the broad expanse around Chimney Bank Top at Rosedale, the view of Eskdale from Lealholm Bank Top, and the panorama of Whitby from the summit of Blue Bank near Sleights. From Ralph Cross between Castleton and Hutton-le-Hole, there is a view of almost 360 degrees, and from Ampleforth Beacon you can see the North York Moors National Park towards the coast, the Dales National Park towards the Pennines and even the Wolds to the south.

There are many more, some well known and others which can be found only by leisurely exploration. These viewpoints draw visitors to the moors, and when people arrive in large numbers, they often cause problems for many people, including village constables.

In the mind of a constable, it is a constant source of amazement that ordinary people can generate so much extraordinary work or create so many complexities as they occupy themselves upon this fair earth. In our quiet moorland villages during those peaceful days in the mid-1960s, we knew that, when the summer season began, usually around Whitsuntide, it would, for a few short months, change the pace of our gentle life. There would be an influx of people, cars and litter. There would be an increase of lost and found property, outbreaks of petty violence and drunkenness, and misadventures by the daft and unprepared, as well as many unforeseen problems. Rarely a week would pass without a blemish of some kind.

These problems have led the moor folk to question the merit of sharing their inheritance with others who care so little for it, and there are times when one wonders if we should attempt to deter those who spoil the blessed tranquillity and beauty of nature's finest places. Perhaps we should increase our efforts to convince outsiders that the whole of Yorkshire is a land of pit-heaps, back-to-back streets and factory chimneys. It's an image we managed to cultivate in the past, and it might prevent the thoughtless and careless from plaguing our landscape.

Such thoughts often occurred to me as I patrolled the more popular parts of the southern aspect of the moors. It was on such a tour of duty, one bright and sunny Sunday in early March, that I was experiencing a cool breeze that brought goosepimples to the flesh and a threat of rain or even snow on the higher ground. It was not the sort of day when you'd expect an influx of tourists but, with Easter close at hand and with some workers using the last of their annual holidays before 31 March, I found that the honeypots of the moors were busier than expected. I think the bright sunshine was responsible – people loved to drive onto the moors in such conditions.

An added bonus was that, after a shower of rain, the clarity of long-distance views was remarkable. Some seemed to stretch almost into infinity, and picnickers would sit in their cars to admire distant places. It gave them the feeling of being on top of the world.

In my official mini-van with its blue light on top, I was enjoying a 9 a.m.–5 p.m. shift, and it didn't escape my notice that I was getting paid to tour the moors while others were having to do so in their own time. During the first few hours, I found little to harass me. I had spent time report-writing in the office at Ashfordly, followed by an hour in Brantsford, where I patrolled the market town on foot as the church bells rang. After this, I decided to drive onto the heights above Lairsbeck, with its scattering of cottages around the tiny chapel. There was a Forestry Commission plantation nearby and, over the months, we had received occasional reports of damage to several units of fire-fighting equipment. These were left unattended around the perimeter of the trees, and we wondered at the mentality of those who destroy or damage life-saving equipment – I would inspect them during my visit. I would also eat my sandwich lunch on the moors. Just like a tourist, I'd find a view of my very own! My decision made, I drove to the top of Bracken Hill. I would park there and enjoy a walk along the heathery ridge with its own fine views of Lairsdale.

Once I was out of the sheltering fabric of the van, the wind was chilling and more than fresh in spite of the sun; a brisk moorland walk would be an excellent appetizer.

And so it was. A leisurely ramble around the plantation showed that the fire-fighting equipment had not been interfered with; this pleased me, and I decided upon a short diversion from the route back to my van. This took me across the open moor, where a skylark was singing and black-faced sheep roamed without hindrance. Up here, there are no fences to contain the sheep: they live almost as wild animals, each instinctively remaining within its own patch of heather or 'heeaf'. 'Heeafed yows' (ewes) are those which are mature enough to remain within their own territory and, at that time of the year, many were carrying unborn lambs. Others had already given birth to delightful black-faced infants, and the tiny lambs were tough enough to survive the bleak conditions which prevailed.

I enjoyed the brisk walk and found myself upon a little-used track which led back to the car-park. As I strode across the heather, moving rapidly to keep warm, I became aware of a Bedford personnel-carrier which was parked on a nab top. A nab is a protruding piece of land. This one overlooked Lairsdale, and the vehicle was positioned so that its passengers could enjoy the views on all sides. Someone had selected the ideal place for a picnic.

As I approached, a large brown-and-white mongrel, the size of a greyhound, leapt from the rear doors. It was fussing about in a state of some excitement and was immediately followed by three laughing children. Dog and children galloped away in a frenzy of barking and shouting, and there seemed to be a large family with the vehicle. As it stood with its rear doors wide open, I could see the wooden seats which ran along each side, with three seats in the front, one of which was the driver's. The driver, a tall man in his fifties, with greying hair, was laughing and calling encouragement to the children and the dog, and at that moment I felt happiness for the family in their exuberance.

But almost immediately that happiness turned to disbelief and shock. The dog began to chase some sheep and lambs. The children encouraged it, laughing and shouting as the frightened animals galloped through the bracken and heather. The mongrel raced in pursuit, clearly enjoying the 'game'.

I expected the grey-haired man to call it off, to make the children stop. But he didn't. He was laughing too. He was curiously enjoying the panic generated in the sheep.

The distressed animals did not know which way to run to escape from the barking dog or the shouting children. Tiny lambs bleated in terror and became separated from their mothers, while panic caused the pregnant ewes to be in danger of aborting. If they did, it would be a costly business for the farmer who owned them, and a traumatic time for the animals. Within moments, the flock had been scattered, and I knew that if this daft dog managed to bite one and taste blood, it could turn into a sheep-killer.

'Hey!' I shouted and ran towards the van. 'Hey, stop that! Call that dog off!'

The grey-haired man turned and saw me. No one had been aware of my presence until that moment. The whole family was clearly surprised and embarrassed at my unexpected arrival. As I shouted in my anger and horror at their stupidity, I noticed another man climb from the van. He was younger than the first and was followed by two women. One was about his own age, and the other might have been his mother or mother-in-law.

'Bonnie, heel!' He looked at me, then at the frenzied dog and immediately appraised the situation. 'John, call Bonnie off, stop him . . .'

But the dog had other ideas. It ignored the calls to heel and bounded through the clumps of heather, seeking more sheep to chase, more lambs to harass. The three children were a long way behind it, too far away to seize it, and so the shouting man had to rely on the authority in his voice.

'Bonnie, heel! Heel, I say! Damn you, heel!'

'I'm sorry, Constable . . .' the older man was at my side. 'I had no idea it would do that . . . I must . . .'

'That dog should be shot!' I snapped at him. 'Of all the crazy things to do, letting it loose like that . . .'

'Bonnie, heel!' the younger man was having some success now. His powerful voice had penetrated the dog's consciousness and halted its mad gallop; it stood with tail wagging and looked at its master, then once more regarded the sheep. At this stage, they had come to a standstill and had assembled at a safe distance to stare stupidly at the dog. It was on the point of repeating its game when its master called again.

'Heel!' he shouted, 'Heel, Bonnie, heel!'

The three children, a boy and two girls in their early teens, now came to the side of the man. The dog came too, wagging its tail and panting in joy.

'Sorry, Dad,' said the boy. 'I thought it was a bit of fun.'

'All right, no harm done,' said the man as the mongrel arrived at his side, its tail wagging half in happiness but half in expectation of trouble. It had recognized the anger in his voice. 'Heel, Bonnie! Sit!'

The dog sat and looked up at him, eyes wide and trusting. Its tongue lolled as it panted heavily from the exercise, and its tail thumped the ground. I was now at the younger man's side, the children hovering at a discreet distance. The older man had been lingering just out of my sight, close to the two women, but now made as if to speak to me . . .

'Er, Constable . . .' He stepped forward, but I was in no mood for excuses. I ignored his interruption.

'Who is the owner of this dog?' I demanded.

'Er, it's mine,' said the younger man.

'For a start, it's not wearing a collar,' I said. 'And that is an offence. The collar should bear your name and address. And it is also an offence to allow a dog to worry livestock – and chasing them is classed as worrying. It means the owner of these sheep could have shot your dog if he'd caught it just now. It also means I can summon you to court for you to give reasons why your dog shouldn't be destroyed at the worst or at the very least kept under control, and it means that, if any damage or injury is done to these sheep, the farmer can claim compensation from you.'

One of the girls started to cry.

'Look, the children would have no idea of the consequences. We're townspeople, we don't understand the seriousness . . . I mean, the dog was just playing . . .'

'The dog was not just playing!' I retorted. 'You people were encouraging it. It was chasing sheep. Some are heavy with unborn lambs and they might have aborted – they still might abort – and that will cost the farmer a lot of money. He might come to you for compensation. This might cost you a lot of money. Now, your name, please.'

'Look, I'm sorry. I'll make sure it never happens again.'

The older man came forward again. 'Look, er, Constable, this is my son-in-law, and he meant no harm. Now, I think . . .'

'Are you the owner of the dog?' I put to the older man.

'No, officer, I am not.'

'Then kindly allow me to speak to the owner. This is *his* responsibility. So,' I continued to address the younger man, 'your name and address, please?'

My notebook was ready. He said his name was John Horwell and gave an address in Wakefield; he was thirty-eight years old and a schoolmaster. I gave him a lecture about general behaviour in the countryside and suggested he make an effort to learn more about rural matters; I said he would be capable of passing his knowledge to the children, both his own and those he taught at school.

I then told him, in very official tones and by invoking the correct procedures, that I was going to report him for: (a) allowing a dog to be in a public place while not wearing a collar bearing the owner's name and address; (b) being the owner of a dog which worried livestock on agricultural land, i.e. the moor. I said that I was going to summon him to appear at court to show cause why an order should not be made for the dog to be kept under proper control.

Whilst I was at it, I also asked for his driving licence and insurance, but as he had none with him, I issued him with the standard form HO/RT/1, which meant he had five clear days to produce them at a police office of his choice. He chose Wakefield. I told him to take his dog licence too.

In throwing the book at Mr Horwell, I was fairly certain that the chief constable would not authorize prosecution on any of these charges; instead, he would probably issue a formal written caution, but it would be a a valuable lesson to the family. I took all their names as possible witnesses.

My concern was that incidents of this kind had to be halted. They were becoming increasingly frequent as more people took their leisure on the moors. I now felt that this family would be more careful, and they would relate their story to friends and neighbours. The long-term deterrent effect would be of some modest benefit to country folk and their livestock.

Having cast gloom and despondency upon their outing, I noted the registration number of the vehicle just in case I had been given a false name and address. Then I departed towards my own vehicle, making a mental note to provide the farmer with details of this incident, should he wish to pursue the matter privately. I was not in any mood to sit near that location for my picnic lunch, so I drove to another viewpoint, there to calm down over my coffee and sandwiches.

When I returned to Ashfordly police office later that afternoon, I completed my paperwork and rang the West Riding Constabulary control room to ask them to check ownership of the Bedford carrier. When I provided the registration number, the girl immediately said, 'It's in our records. It belongs to Mr Laurence Nelson,' and she gave me his address.

'Nelson?' the name triggered some kind of memory deep in my mind, but its significance eluded me.

'Yes,' she said. 'He's the chief constable of Holbeck County Borough Force.'

I groaned. A chief constable! I had almost booked a chief constable! But he should have known better! Nonetheless, I wondered how he would view my behaviour during those fraught moments. I wondered if he would be critical of my actions, whether I had done everything according to the book or whether I had exceeded my authority. And I wondered what Sergeant Blaketon would do with my report when I concluded it with the sentence, 'Mr Horwell is the son-in-law of Mr Laurence Nelson, chief constable of Holbeck County Borough Police Force. Mr Nelson was present during my interview of the defendant.'

I was to learn later that Horwell was given a written caution for each of his transgressions, which I felt was quite adequate.

I heard nothing from Mr Laurence Nelson and don't know whether he ever contacted any of my superiors.

As a matter of historical record, some years later his tiny police force was absorbed into the surrounding county constabulary as a result of boundary changes, and it no longer exists.

While the splendid heights attracted the multitudes, so did the lush green dales and the pretty stone-built villages. They drew an increasingly mobile public from the humdrum existence of dingy city streets and the conformity of semi-detached suburbia. Quite suddenly, the splendour of the Yorkshire landscape was available to all. The influx surprised those of us who lived and worked in the more remote and attractive districts.

This was in direct contrast to pre-war days. Then, the occasional visitor would pass through a village, perhaps halting for a drink and a chat at the village inn, but by the mid-1960s they were coming in their thousands. Some came by coachload, others came on foot or by bicycle, but mostly they came by car. I think it is fair comment that our villages, and even the charming market towns, were unprepared for this onslaught upon their amenities. There were few car-parking facilities, no public toilets, a definite shortage of places to halt for a soft drink or cup of tea, and a dearth of information directed specifically at visitors.

Many had no idea how to behave in the countryside – they left gates open, which caused cattle and horses to stray, sometimes with fatal consequences; they regarded all fields, whether crop-bearing or not, as common land; they left their rubbish and litter; they picked wild flowers to the point of rarity, and some even chopped up wooden fences to light fires or demolished dry stone walls in their determination to take home a piece of moorland granite to start a rockery. There was ingratitude, ignorance and vandalism on a scale hitherto unknown.

But the people of the moors learned to cope. Some saw the financial advantages of this perpetual influx and opened cafés, caravan sites and bed-and-breakfast establishments, while those in authority were forced to plan for this expanding tourist industry. Car-parks appeared, direction signs proliferated, information packs were compiled and byelaws created, all to regulate the increasing flow of visitors and protect the countryside and its inhabitants.

One pretty dale received more than its fair share; tens of thousands of visitors swarmed along its narrow, hilly lanes. The snag was that most of them arrived at the same time. They were not spread out across the year or even the summer season as were other places – they were compressed into a couple of weekends every year, usually around Easter.

The outcome was that the police were duty-bound to sort out the traffic confusion created by thousands of cars on lanes far too narrow, winding and steep to accommodate the width or length of a bus. It was a recipe for chaos. Just add a stubborn tractor-driver or shepherd with his flock, and the mixture could become volatile. The result could be a traffic jam several miles long – and this was in the days long before the M1 or the M25 and their notorious blockages.

The short-lived attraction was wild daffodils. There were hundreds of thousands of them, even millions, and they grew (and still grow) in splendid and colourful profusion along the banks of the River Dove in Farndale. There are miles of them, and they add a unique charm to this delightful moorland dale. The dale is also known for its thatched cottages and cruck houses, as well as its remoteness and splendid upland views, but it was the wild daffodils which first attracted the crowds.

Topographical books published before the turn of this century omitted references to these flowers, but once news of their presence did circulate, it brought in the thieves and vandals. They all wanted summat for nowt.

Greedy visitors came with scissors, scythes, sickles, trowels, spades and wheelbarrows and began to dig up the bulbs or cut barrowloads of flowers to sell in local city markets. Such was the threat from these looters that in 1953 the dale was made a local nature reserve, with a byelaw to protect the flowers.

And so the police officers whose duty took them to Farndale had two prime tasks – one was to control traffic, and the other was to protect the flowers, although there were also such ancillary tasks as first aid, lost and found property, missing children and wandering old ladies, thefts, vehicle breakdowns, lost dogs, litter and that host of other problems that are generated when crowds assemble.

Daffodil Duty, as we termed it, was one of my regular tasks, although Farndale was not on my own beat. Like the other officers in the area, I was diverted to Farndale from time to time, and it was a busy, if enjoyable task. Five or six constables, a sergeant and some special constables were drafted in when the daffodils bloomed. Our brief was simple – it was to keep the traffic moving.

Fortunately, although the roads were narrow, steep and winding, they did have one advantage: they formed a figure 8 as they wove around the dale. There was a tiny car-park near the central length of that figure 8, and if a one-way traffic system was instituted around the loops, it would prevent blockages. But only half the figure 8 (the lower half) was wide enough to cope with buses – and buses came by the score. On the main approach roads, signs were erected to guide coaches along one specific route: they must drive up the right-hand side of the lower dale, turn left along the link road and disgorge their passengers, and then park on the return leg of the bottom of the figure 8. That lane was wide enough to permit coaches to park, and when their passengers regained them, they could drive out of the dale without problems. Coaches had not to enter the top half of the figure 8.

Private cars, on the other hand, could cope with the steep, narrow lanes around the top half of that figure 8 (even if some of their drivers couldn't!). However, this could operate only on a one-way system. There was no space for large numbers of cars to pass or overtake each other. We created a system whereby they entered the dale via the same route as the coaches and were directed by a policeman on traffic duty across to the left of the dale. They then drove up the left of the top of the figure 8 and circled the dale to return to the centre, where they encountered the same policeman. There they were fed into the incoming stream of cars to cross the 8 in the middle, and then they could leave the dale down the left hand leg. (They could not leave via the right-hand leg because the incoming buses filled the roads.) And with good nature from all, and a capable policeman on that central road of the figure 8, it worked. Traffic on that central stretch must be kept moving.

Understandably, some of the local residents and farmers did not relish a full tour of the dale to post a letter or gain access to their own premises. In time, we got to know them and their foibles and so would halt the traffic to allow a local person to go against the flow.

This was not always a success, however, because inevitably some obstreperous motorist would demand to go the same way, having seen us treat the locals with some sympathy. Initially, we explained our actions to those who grumbled, but too many wanted special treatment. After a time our patience was exhausted, so we never explained or argued with such drivers – if they were very awkward, they found themselves doing a longer than usual tour. The total round trip was in the region of eleven miles, but with a spot of collusion from other constables, awkward and inconsiderate drivers could find themselves doing a long second trip.

The truly tricky bit, from a traffic-control point of view, was the central part of that figure 8. All traffic used that short stretch of road whether entering or leaving the dale. Traffic new to the dale, both buses and cars, was channelled along it, but cars which had toured the top of the dale were also channelled along it as they were guided to their exit route. So long as everyone kept moving, knew where they were heading and did as they were told, there was no trouble. Even so, it required a good and patient constable to cope with the never-ending problems at that very important point. A blockage there would halt the entire dale, something of no great consequence to tourists but of very serious consideration if it prevented access by emergency vehicles, such as ambulances, fire appliances and doctors' cars.

I recall one such problem. A coach had overshot the junction by about ten yards and needed to reverse in order to get around the bend into its correct route. But in those few moments other cars had arrived and were now queuing behind it. If each one reversed a short distance, the problem would be solved – the coach could move backwards, giving it space to turn the corner and then be on its way. But when I put this to the lady driving the car immediately behind it, she said haughtily, 'Officer, I never reverse!'

'But, madam,' I replied, 'if you don't, the entire dale will be blocked. All I'm asking is for you to move back to that gate . . . a few yards . . . then the bus can proceed.'

'I have told you, Constable. I never reverse. Never!'

I could have argued all day and threatened her with prosecution for obstructing the highway, but none of that would solve the immediate crisis. Already more cars were heading this way – if we didn't get her moving soon, there would be a massive blockage.

'Would you mind if I moved it for you?' I asked.

'Not at all.' She was a picture of charm and, I suspect, some relief as I reversed her little Austin for the necessary distance.

That hiccup was of little consequence in comparison with the traffic jam created there one Easter Sunday afternoon at the peak of the influx of vehicles.

We had a new constable with us. He had transferred from Leeds City Police because his wife hated town life, and he had been posted to Eltering. His name was David Parry; he had about eight years service and was soon trying to impress us with stories of his daring exploits in policing a city, especially around the Saturday night trouble-spots as the pubs turned out. We got the impression he had controlled the entire centre of Leeds single-handed, and he adapted his boasting to the situation when he was earmarked for Daffodil Duty in Farndale. As we assembled in the village hall for briefing and allocation of points, he boasted that this traffic duty was nothing compared with rush hour on The Headrow at Leeds, one of the busiest thoroughfares in the city.

'I can do the Headrow with my eyes shut,' he said that Easter Sunday morning. 'Multiple lanes, traffic lights, junctions to cope with . . . crowds . . . lorries and buses . . . that was a piece of cake. What have you here, then? A few buses and cars – mebbe a tractor or two? All on the same road? It's a country lane – it'll be a doddle.'

'I'm delighted that we have such an expert amongst us,' beamed Sergeant Bairstow with his customary good nature. 'So, David, maybe you'd do the central stretch? That bit definitely needs the skills of an expert point-duty man.'

Bairstow explained the requirements and the likely problems, then showed PC Parry the link road at the junction of the figure 8.

'Nothing to it, Sarge!' beamed Parry as he warmed to the task of showing us country cousins how to do a proper job.

'Nick.' The sergeant turned to me. 'You've done this before; you take this car-park. Stop 'em parking here except for disgorging passengers. And relieve David as and when necessary. Explain your job to him before you hand over. OK?'

'Fine, Sarge,' I smiled.

After a cup of coffee, we went to our posts. It was a dull April morning, with clouds threatening rain, and we wondered if the weather would deter the visitors. We felt it would not. Many would already have made plans or even left home by now. For the first hour or so, however, very few vehicles arrived, and I knew that PC Parry would find this boring in the extreme. But as lunch time approached, the clouds evaporated, a warm breeze appeared from the west, and the April sun beamed upon the dale. And the daffodils opened their trumpet-shaped blooms to welcome the incoming visitors as they began to arrive by the hundred and even the thousand.

Quite suddenly, the dale was transformed. From my vantage-point on the car-park, I could see the procession of oncoming buses and cars. It stretched way out of sight. The constable at the first junction was feeding them across to PC Parry, who in turn was dividing the buses and cars. The cars were being sent towards me; some disgorged their passengers and went on to park higher in the dale. Others completed a circular tour before returning later for their passengers.

By two o'clock the dale was filled with moving vehicles, but I began to realize that their progress was slowing. Quite suddenly, things went wrong. Within minutes traffic in the dale was grinding to a halt. The queue of buses waiting to disgorge passengers was growing, and then, as I looked across the dale to the junction at the far side, I could see that the traffic was stationary for a long way back. Nothing was moving. No cars were passing my point. They were backed for miles down the far side . . . and there was a queue from both the upper and lower dale . . . outgoing cars had been brought to a halt and so had incoming vehicles. The entire dale, miles and miles of it, was at a standstill and the air was was beginning to fill with the ghastly music of the great British motoring public – they were tooting their car horns. It sounded like the centre of Paris . . .

The blockage could only be at PC Parry's point. Sergeant Bairstow was up the dale, so I decided to investigate. After all, Parry's point was only a few yards from mine, although beyond my line of vision. When I arrived, I found mayhem. Cars and buses were jammed at his point; a bus was stuck across the road, there was a tractor and trailer trying to manœuvre past them, and cars were queuing patiently to get past them all. Some drivers were out of their cars, arguing, others were blowing their horns, and some bus passengers had disembarked to march steadfastly towards the daffodils. And in the middle of the road there was PC Parry.

He was on his knees. His hands were covering his head, which was bare. His cap was lying a few yards away, and he held his head close to the surface of the road. I could see by the movements of his body that he was in great distress and appeared to be weeping. I ran to help him, assisting him to his feet and placing him momentarily in a house doorway as uncontrollable tears flowed down his face. Then, with the aid of two bus-drivers, I organized some shunting of buses and cars, a telling-off for the tractor-driver, and after some ten minutes and a lot of shouting, we got things moving again. Eventually the cars filtered towards the higher dale, and the buses went to their parking spaces. The horn-honking faded away as the traffic began to move.

But I had David Parry to deal with. I asked one level-headed motorist to give PC Parry a lift to the village hall, and as he did so, I radioed for Sergeant Bairstow to come and look at his ailing constable.

'I think he needs treatment, Sarge,' I said into my radio. 'But I'm not sure what his problem is.'

'I'll see to him, Nick,' came the response.

I stood on the busy road, guiding buses and cars to their correct destinations, and then an ambulance arrived. It manœuvred itself through the throng of incoming traffic and eventually rushed off to Brantsford Cottage Hospital with PC Parry inside.

That Daffodil Duty became a very busy one, and as we ended our duty at six o'clock that evening, Sergeant Bairstow thanked us all. It had been a record turn-out, so he thought – but tomorrow was still to come.

'Same again tomorrow, lads,' he smiled. 'Same points. Easter Monday will be busy – the weather forecast says it'll be fine and sunny, like today.'

'What about PC Parry, Sarge?' I asked. 'How is he?'

'He's fine now, thanks, Nick,' smiled Bairstow. 'They've sent him home. But we're replacing him for tomorrow's duties. We shan't be using him again for Daffodil Duty.'

'Are our country drivers too much for him?' asked one of the constables.

'No, it's the daffodils,' laughed Bairstow. 'It seems he's allergic to them. The pollen got to him . . . he sneezed himself silly . . .'

'That's flower power,' chuckled some wag as we prepared to leave.

2 *Life's Little Mysteries*

> Like one that on a lonesome road
> Doth walk in fear and dread,
> And having once turned round walks on,
> And turns no more his head.
>
> Samuel Taylor Coleridge (1772–1834)

It requires the knowledge of a local person to make full use of the interconnecting network of minor roads which pattern the heights and dales of the North York Moors. Businessfolk and visitors tend to use the A- or B-class routes, even though only one A-class road runs north to south across the moors. That is the A169 from Whitby to Pickering. The A171 crosses the northern moors from west to east as it runs from Guisborough to Scarborough; it visits Whitby, then hugs the picturesque coastline as it turns towards the Queen of Watering Places. Another main road, the A174, touches the very northernmost part of the moors between Staithes and Whitby, while the A172/173 lie over to the west. There are no other A-class roads, although the B1257, with its panoramic views, runs down Bilsdale from Stokesley to Helmsley. This is the only B-class road completely to traverse the heights.

This dearth of main roads is compensated by a bewildering network of unclassified routes. They run down the dales or snake across the moors to link dale with dale or village with village. In addition, there are hundreds of miles of ancient tracks, green lanes, disused roads and bridleways, and these do tend to be well used by the moorfolk, especially when the main roads are busy with summer traffic.

A large-scale map will help identify these, but in general terms they are beyond the sights of the casual visitor. However, one moorland road is centuries older than any of these, and it has been discovered by the tourists.

It is the Roman road which crosses Wheeldale Moor near Goathland. Alternatively known as 'T'Aud Wife's Trod' or 'Wade's Causeway', ancient legend said it was built by the giant Wade and his wife Bell who had to cross the moors between Mulgrave Castle and Pickering Castle. More professional examination proved it to be of great historical importance and antiquity, because it was found to be a genuine Roman road and not the work of a legendary giant. It is the only Roman road known to have entered this part of North Yorkshire and is the finest example of its type in Britain. Six hundred feet above sea-level, the uncovered portion extends about a mile and a quarter, and it is a remarkable feat of construction. Sixteen feet wide and made up of flat stones on a bed of gravel, it is raised in the centre to facilitate drainage and even has side gutters and culverts.

It is even more remarkable when we realize that some of our own roads were little more than mud tracks even into this century. It required a man like John MacAdam (1756–1836) to emulate this style many centuries later. The Roman road has survived almost twenty centuries on this bleak and windswept moorland, and it is sad to record that some of it has been ploughed up, and some stones have been plundered for house-building, while others have been utilized in the construction of the present road from Stape to Egton Bridge. Fortunately, this fine stretch has survived.

In my routine patrols as the village constable of Aidensfield, I had little cause to visit the Roman road, but my wife and I had taken the children to see it during one of my days off duty. It was not on my patch, although it did lie on the boundaries of the division in which I was stationed. For this reason, it was perfectly feasible that sooner or later I should have to deal with an incident up there. It happened one miserable, wet and foggy day in June and was to prove a most interesting and curious day's work.

Even the initial inquiry contained a certain air of mystery. I was instructed to visit Ravenstone Farm on the edge of Wheeldale Moor, and there examine a tractor being used by the tenant farmer, a Mr Stanley Bayley. As the farm was very remote, I was provided with a map reference and was told that it overlooked Wheeldale Gill and that the road to it was rather rough.

'Understood,' I responded. 'But what is the purpose of this vehicle-examination?'

'We have received an anonymous call,' Control informed me. 'It suggests we examine the tractor being used at that address. No further details were given. The caller rang off. Over.'

'Ten four.' I gave the formal acknowledgement of the message and set about my task. This meant a rough drive along forest tracks, and it would be around noon when I reached the edge of Wheeldale Moor.

By now, the entire landscape was obliterated by a thick moorland fog, a 'roak' as it was locally known. Damp, wet and clinging, it deadened all the sounds of the moors as it eerily enveloped my little van. With headlights blazing, I chugged and bounced along the track. It was slow progress, for the road was rutted with deep holes and puddles; huge, bare stones protruded at intervals and threatened to tear off my exhaust system, and at times I had to drive onto the turf to circumnavigate a particularly rough stretch. I passed the southern tip of the Roman road and began to wonder if I was approaching the right place but a check on the map proved I was right. By 12.15, therefore, in clinging fog, I turned along a farm track, crossed a cattle grid and found myself in a farmyard which appeared to be full of brown hens, broken-down farm waggons and derelict implements.

There was no sign of human habitation.

In the clinging mist, the entire premises looked like a deserted homestead from a Gothic novel. A zinc bath full of water stood in the yard, with a goose on guard – it honked at my approach, but no one appeared; a rusting reaper stood abandoned in one corner, and several old ploughs and iron tractor wheels littered the yard. A thin, dirty cat peered at me from beneath a wooden trough, then scuttled away into an outbuilding, frightened when my foot kicked an empty tin. As I surveyed this desolate spot, I began to wonder if I was the victim of some kind of prank. Determined to find an answer, I made for the door of the house. It needed a few coats of paint, and there was no lock; it was held shut with a piece of string. There was a hole where the knob should be.

I rapped as loudly as I could, and shouted, 'Anybody there?'

With some surprise and relief, I did get a response. Inside the house, I heard a door open and soon a man opened the door. In his late thirties and about my height, he was dressed in work clothes and smelled of cows; he had not shaved for days, his fair hair was matted and dank, and his hands were ingrained with the filth of months.

'Oh,' he said. 'The law.'

'Mr Bayley?'

'Aye,' he said, not inviting me in.

'Can I see your tractor?' I asked.

'What for?' he put to me.

I laughed. 'Look, I don't know. I've been instructed to examine it.' I hoped my own puzzlement would soften him. 'Our office got an anonymous call . . .'

'There's some nosey buggers about. It'll be some o' them hikers we get in. They get lost, they come here looking for help . . . Come on, then, follow me. It's in t'shed. It *is* taxed, thoo knows.'

He led me across the untidy yard into a dry building which was open on one side. The interior of the shed was even more untidy than the exterior, being filled with empty sacks and oil drums, but a small tractor was parked in one of the bays.

'There she is,' he said, with a certain pride in his voice. 'Grand little lass is yon.'

It was. It was a lovely little Fergie, as these tiny Ferguson tractors were called. Painted a pleasing grey, it was surprisingly clean and well maintained. I guessed it was of the 1950s era. It had an exhaust which rose from the engine like a chimney, which meant it could operate in deep water. Huge semi-circular mudguards covered the giant rear wheels. I found the tax disc and noted it was up-to-date, so I still wondered why I was staring at this delightful machine. And then, as I walked to the rear of it, I knew.

The seat was wrong. I remembered these tractors having a metal seat which was shaped to accommodate the backside of an average farmworker; with holes for ventilation, each seat was mounted on a tough horseshoe-shaped spring of steel. This gave some comfort to the roughest ride. But this tractor had no such seat. Instead, it bore an enormous and totally strange contraption with coloured wires and plastic pipes. It took only seconds for me to recognize it as a pilot's ejector seat from a jet aircraft. As I stared at it, I recalled a crash on these moors several months ago. The pilot had been killed . . . wreckage had been strewn for miles.

'This seat?' I asked him.

'Aye, Ah kem across it ower t'moor,' he said. 'Frev yon jet that crashed a while back . . . doon in t'gill, t'seat was, it had flown hundreds o' yards from t'plane. Them RAF fellers never found it, so Ah thought it would be grand for me.'

And so, with some skilful adaptations and a spot of home welding, he had secured it to his tractor.

When I took a closer look, I was horrified.

'Good God, Mr Bayley!' I exclaimed as I scrutinized his very grand tractor seat. 'This one is alive!'

'Alive?' he looked puzzled.

'It's an ejector seat,' I explained. 'When a pilot is crashing, he pulls a lever which detonates an explosive charge under this seat. That shoots off the canopy and propels the seat from the plane – with the pilot in it. Then he's supposed to separate from it and parachute to safety. But this pilot didn't manage that, did he? He didn't eject. He was thrown out and killed, remember?'

'Aye.'

'So when the plane crashed, this seat must have been flung far enough . . . and it's still full of explosive! See . . . the firing pin's not been used. Now, whatever you do, don't touch it. I'll make it safe.'

'Dis thoo mean ti say Ah've been sittin' on yon pack o' gunpowder and Ah could have been blown sky high?'

'That's exactly what I'm saying, Mr Bayley.'

The expression on his face was a joy to behold. Fortunately, police officers are instructed on the safe methods of dealing with ejector seats, and I knew exactly how to secure this one. I found the safety pin with its red label tucked into a side pocket and slipped it into position. Now the seat was safe; it would not explode. I found it amazing that it had survived intact like this.

'What would really 'ave 'appened if yon thing 'ad gone off wi' me sitting on it?' he asked, still brooding over my initial comments.

'I meant what I said,' I told him. 'It would have sent you hundreds of feet into the sky.' I had to laugh now. 'But with no parachute, you'd have come down with one hell of a bump – and the chances are you would have broken your back on landing, or maybe your neck in the process of being launched. In short, you could have been killed, Mr Bayley. Pilots are trained to use those seats – tractor-drivers aren't.'

'But thoo'll not be arresting me for pinching it?'

'No,' I said. 'I've received no complaint about a theft. Besides, it was lost. But I think I'd better call the RAF to come and remove the explosive charges, to make it safe. They might let you keep the seat.'

'Thanks,' he said with feeling, that feeling being one of relief.

'It's thanks to the anonymous caller,' I reminded him. 'Mebbe hikers aren't such a nuisance?'

'Mebbe not,' he grinned suddenly. 'Ah might let 'em sleep in my barn from now on. Now, is thoo coming in for a drink, then?'

'Aye,' I said.

I first called the office on my radio and explained the problem. The duty sergeant said he would request the RAF to deal with the seat. I was then accompanied into the house and, in the custom of the moors, was invited to sit down for dinner, as lunch is called hereabouts. In spite of the state of the exterior, the kitchen was a model of cleanliness, thanks to the busy Mrs Bayley, and the meal was superb.

I left the farm an hour later, having sampled a tiny drop of the Bayley's home-made beer. As I drove, I did wonder what on earth would have happened if that seat had launched Mr Bayley from his little Fergie. If nothing else, it would have surprised the grouse population, and I did wonder if Mr Bayley had ever flown . . .

But my day's duty was not over. As I was returning along the pot-holed track beyond the farm, a middle-aged man hailed me. Clad in overalls and sporting a flat cap, he appeared out of the mist, which was now thinning but still of considerable density, and he waved me to a halt.

'Ah saw you go up Ravenstone way,' he said as I climbed out. 'Ah thought Ah'd better wait and catch you on t'way back.'

'Summat wrong?' I asked.

'Aye,' he said. He explained that his name was Ernie Smallwood and that he was the warden for the Roman road, employed by the Ministry of Works. His job was to maintain the ancient road and keep it safe from modern predators. Then he told me, 'There's a chap sitting in my 'ut. Ah can't get a word o' sense out of 'im.'

'Who is he?' I asked. 'One of your workmen?'

'Nay, lad, there's only me works this road. Ah think 'e's a 'iker got lost. Ah reckon 'e doesn't know where 'e is. 'E sounds a bit daft to me.'

'Is he injured?' I was contemplating the need for an ambulance and could call one via the radio before venturing along this ancient highway.

'No, 'e doesn't seem 'urt, just dazed.'

'Right, I'll come and have a look at him.'

Ernie led me along the uneven surface of this amazing road; perhaps it had once been smooth enough for chariots, but the ravages of centuries had rendered it rough and undulating. Nonetheless, the craftsmanship in its construction was evident, and I was very conscious that I was walking along a road built for the use of Roman soldiers about a century after Christ. The sense of history was almost overwhelming.

Ernie took me to his hut, which was a small wooden building like a garden shed. Perched on the moor beside the Roman road and overlooking one of the streams which trickled into Wheeldale Beck, it was painted dark green to blend with the moors. Behind it was a partition which contained a basic toilet, but the hut had no electricity or water, although it did provide a modicum of shelter and rest during Ernie's lonely working hours. His bike was propped against the outside, and inside was a pair of old armchairs, a Calor-gas ring, kettle and tea-making equipment, along with a few other comforts such as paperbacks, magazines and tins of sweets. I also noticed some little carved stone animals. I was to learn that Ernie whiled away his time by sculpting animals from pieces of moorland stone – but he never used any from the road in his care! I spotted a realistic badger and squirrel among them.

Sitting in one of the armchairs was a pale, haggard man in his early thirties. A rucksack stood on the floor at his side; I saw it had a rolled-up sleeping-bag secured to the top. He was clad in hiking gear – large, well-oiled boots, thick socks and adequate sweaters completed his outfit, and he wore a white woolly hat. I could see strands of fair hair sticking from beneath it, around his ears and neck, and his pale blue eyes looked frightened and nervous. He sat almost as if he was in a stupor, and his hands were clasped on his lap. He had the typical appearance of a man in a state of shock.

'Hello.' I stood before him. 'I'm PC Rhea, one of the local policemen. Can I help you?'

There was no response; it was as if he had not heard my voice. I tried again, but the outcome was the same.

'E's been like that since 'e got here,' said Ernie, who stood at the door. 'Not a word 'as 'e said. Nowt.'

I knew that one good remedy for shock was a cup of hot, sweet tea, so I asked Ernie if he would brew one. He smiled and agreed, going down to the beck to fill his kettle with pure moorland water. Soon it was singing on his gas ring. Although I repeatedly tried to make contact with the hiker, I got no response. Eventually I thrust a mug of tea into his hands and was pleased when he accepted it. He began to sip. I felt we had achieved a breakthrough!

'Was he here when you got to work, Ernie?'

'Not then,' he said. 'Ah got 'ere at eight, and there was no sign of 'im. Then Ah went along t'road, towards t'south end; it was my morning check, like Ah do every morning. Ah got back only a short while ago, for my dinner break. 'E was here then. Ah never lock t'doors, t'shed's allus available in a storm. This lad was sitting there, just like 'e is now.'

I joined Ernie and the silent visitor in this most traditional of English rituals and was pleased to see that the fellow did lift the mug to his lips and drink. Ernie allowed me to use the other chair, and as we waited for the lad to recover, Ernie told me about his lonely task. I thought it must be the most curious job in Great Britain, being the lengthman on a Roman road. During this chat, I did not address the youth but did notice that he drank every drop of tea and that our calm chatter in his presence did seem to have created a new awareness in him.

'Thanks,' he said suddenly and without warning. He placed the empty mug on Ernie's shelf. 'Look, I'm sorry . . .'

'That's OK, so long as you're safe and well,' I said. 'Can I give you a lift anywhere? I'm heading back through Brantsford and Ashfordly.'

'Where am I now?' The lad blinked and took several deep breaths, exhaling long, loud rushes of air. It was as if he'd emerged from a coma.

'Wheeldale Moor,' I said.

'I got lost last night, in the fog,' he volunteered. 'I was terrified . . . I must have walked all night . . . It was near dawn when I lay down near one of those streams but it was too cold . . . Then I found this old track and guessed it must lead somewhere. I walked along it, but was worn out, so I sat down for a rest, up there somewhere,' and he waved his hands to indicate a distant part of the old road.

After a pause, he continued: 'And then I went to sleep, I think; I had a funny dream . . . it frightened me. Then, this morning, after I woke up, I found this little shed and came in for a rest . . . I was shattered, really shattered . . . I hadn't a clue where I was, out here . . .'

'There's a youth hostel further across the moor,' I told him.

'I wasn't looking for hostels. I thought I could walk up here and find somewhere to sleep overnight, somewhere in the open, then make my way back today. Anyway, I'm safe.'

'Will anyone be looking for you?' I asked, wondering whether a search had already been instigated.

He shook his head. 'I doubt it. Look, could I have another cup of tea? I'm as dry as a bone . . .'

Ernie obliged. The lad went on to say he lived in Essex but was working on the railways, helping to plan the removal of the tracks along those lines which were to be closed following the 1963 Beeching Report. He had always wanted to see the moors but had had no idea they were so vast and that they could be so inhospitable in the middle of summer.

Now he was chattering quite amiably to Ernie and expressed surprise when Ernie said he'd never been on a train. I knew that was quite feasible – there were people on these moors who had never been out of their own dale, let alone on a train journey.

'Look, I'm sorry,' he went on. 'You must have thought I was odd . . . but, well, I was absolutely whacked, shocked rigid after last night. That tea worked wonders.'

'I'd better have you checked at a hospital,' I suggested. 'Shock is a funny thing.'

'No, it's not the fact I got lost,' he said quietly. 'It was my dream . . . well, I don't think it was a dream. I still can't believe it. Something woke me up, a noise I think, at dawn, and I remember sitting on this old track . . .'

'What happened?' I asked.

'Well, you might think I've been drinking or something, but I swear I haven't. I've got to tell somebody. I can't stop thinking about it. I'd been asleep, literally where I lay, even without my sleeping-bag, and this noise woke me. It was just breaking daylight, and it was misty, not as thick as it was later on, but quite hazy. I heard the noise. It was horses and carts, I thought . . .'

He paused and I could see perspiration on his pale forehead. This was clearly an effort. I wondered what kind of experience could have put him into such a state of shock. Then Ernie winked at me – I had no idea why, but we did not actively persuade the youth to continue. We allowed him to proceed at his own pace as he sipped the second mug of tea. Then he went on with his tale.

'Well, I sat up. I was still on that old road, near the edge, and very tired. I'm sure I was awake . . . anyway, I looked into the mist, thinking it was a local farmer coming along but there were these two chariots . . . racing . . . four horses on each one . . . a man driving each, one with a red tunic and one with a green one . . . they had helmets on and were whipping the horses towards me. Well, I dived out of the way and they came swishing past. I could hear a crowd cheering somewhere in the mist. The noise of the chariot wheels was amazing, rattling along those rough stones on that track out there, and the men, cursing in a language I couldn't understand . . . the horses panting, harness rattling . . .'

'And they disappeared into t'roak?' suggested Ernie.

'Roak?' the lad was puzzled.

'Fog, the morning mist.'

'Yes, they did. I mean, I know I wasn't asleep, I know I was awake, but they don't have chariot races up here, do they?'

'Now and again,' said Ernie slowly. 'Ah've seen 'em, and others has, who live up here. Just like you said.'

'Really?' The lad's eyes brightened. 'Then I wasn't dreaming?'

'No, you saw a chariot race,' said Ernie. 'They used to 'ave 'em along this road – there's a slope just a bit further along. T'spectators used to stand there and cheer. They did 'ave four horses, sometimes six, yoked up in their chariot races, but two as a rule, in war and in normal manœuvres . . .'

'But who are they?'

'The Romans,' said Ernie with all seriousness. 'This is a Roman road, tha knows.'

The lad looked horrified. 'You're joking?'

'No,' said Ernie, lifting a Ministry of Works leaflet from a shelf and passing it to him. 'It's my job to tend it. You saw t'chariot race. Ah've seen it and so have others, but nobody talks about it.'

'But I don't believe in ghosts . . .'

'Me neither,' said Ernie. 'At least, not till I saw yon race.'

'If I tell my mates about this, they'll think I'm crackers,' said the youth, now laughing with the relief that came from the fact that someone did believe him. 'I mean, ghosts don't exist, do they? They can't . . . But those chariots? Surely it would be some local lads doing it for a laugh? I mean, I heard the noise, the rattling, the horses panting, the cheering, I saw the men cursing and whipping their horses . . . I had to dive out of their way . . .'

'You 'ave a look in t'soft bits of ground between them stones out there and try and find t'wheel marks,' challenged Ernie. We all knew there would be none.

Ernie's account of the chariot race was identical with that of the lad, whose name was Ian Jarvis, and he told it in a most practical manner. He said the race usually heralded a time of peril for England – they'd appeared in 1805 before Nelson's death at Trafalgar. They'd also appeared before each of the two world wars – and shortly after Ian's sighting, a Labour government was elected! By the time Ernie had finished his story, Ian Jarvis accepted he had seen a Roman chariot race, but he did not try to understand how or why.

I gave him a lift into Brantsford, and he now seemed fully recovered; he caught a bus back to Malton.

Several weeks later, I learned he had invited Ernie on a train ride from Malton to the Brontë country, which Ernie had always wanted to visit. They were two men who had shared a curious experience – or was it merely a dream? No one talks of the chariots any more, but I often wonder whether they still race across Wheeldale Moor at the crack of dawn.

On another occasion, I had to deal with a lengthman who cared for a stretch of modern moorland road. His name was Rodney James Featherstonehaugh, and he had been the Aidensfield roadman for some twenty years. During my time there, he was nearing retirement, and although others of his kind were being detailed to work in road gangs, Rodney was left alone to end his career around the village he loved. And he did a good job. He was responsible for the lanes around Aidensfield, Elsinby, Briggsby, Ploatby, Waindale, Lairsbeck, Maddleskirk and Crampton. He worked completely alone, although he was answerable to some distant and anonymous boss in the local Highways Department.

I was never sure how Rodney received his instructions or list of duties for the week, or whether any of his superiors ever came to visit him or inspect his work. But his work was immaculate. Without supervision, Rodney kept our lanes and byways in a state of near perfection. He gritted and sanded them in winter, dug out snow drifts or cleared gutters; he weeded the edges, trimmed the verges, clipped overgrown hedges and made sure all the road signs were maintained in a clean and legible state. Nothing seemed to be too much trouble. He was at his best during the winter, when he had an uncanny knack of anticipating frost and snow. Then he would be out at dawn, digging a route through the drifts or scattering salt on the icy stretches which caused the most difficulties.

The snag with a man like Rodney is that no one really appreciates him until he's gone. When he retired, he was missed – in fact, with oceans of goodwill, he would sometimes turn out in his own time, merely to clear a drain or salt a hill which was causing problems. He was that sort of man. His work was his life, and he loved the roads for which he had cared for so long. He knew every inch of them, their history, their weak points, the places liable to frost pockets or flooding. In short, Rodney was irreplaceable.

When he retired, no one took his place. The villages, through private individuals and formal representations by the parish councils, appealed for a replacement, but their pleas were ignored. The council said its team of highway operatives would maintain the roads with just the same care and to the same standard, but of course they could not and did not. Floods developed, drains were blocked, weeds grew apace, the verges thrived until they obstructed corners and blocked views. Rodney had made his mark on our locality.

I came across him quite frequently during my patrols, and I would always stop for a chat. We had a good understanding of one another's duties and areas of responsibility, and if I spotted something which needed his attention, such as a pot hole, damage to a direction sign or the emergence of a spring through the middle of the road, I would inform Rodney and he would do something about it. Similarly, if he knew there were to be roadworks in the area, such as occurred when laying a new surface or digging up a road to lay water mains or telephone lines, he would tell me. I felt that between us we provided a useful public service.

Rodney was very recognizable, even at a great distance. At times, I parked on some of our loftier ridges and saw his dark figure busy with his brush and shovel some miles down the dale. For some reason, he always wore black, which was surprisingly visible in daylight; he had a long black coat, like an army greatcoat, which he wore both summer and winter. His headgear was like a baseball player's cap, and in winter he wore black leather leggings over his stout and studded leather boots.

He pushed a council barrow around too. It was on two wheels, as the dustcarts of our cities used to be, and was really a dustbin on a pair of old car wheels. I think he had made it himself. He used it to contain the rubbish he collected, and it carried his tools – his huge, stiff brush, the shovel, a rod for clearing drains, a hammer and other essentials.

It was some time before I realized what he looked like beneath all that gear. Once I saw him in the Hopbind Inn at Elsinby, and it was a while before I realized that the swarthy, smart man at the bar was Rodney. Like his clothing, he was dark. He had a head of rich black hair with just a hint of grey; his eyebrows were black too, and so were his eyes. He had a black moustache and was swarthy and dark skinned, not through a suntan but through his ancestors. I sometimes wondered if he had gypsy blood in his veins, or whether some of his ancestors came from Spain or Italy.

I liked him. I found him totally honest and reliable, meticulous in his work and always good-humoured and willing in both his private and professional duties. Oddly enough, I never did discover whether he was married or had a family, for he never spoke about his home interests.

But of all the facets of Rodney Featherstonehaugh, the one which most intrigued me was his devotion to time-keeping.

From time to time when I was on patrol, I would see him sitting in the hedge bottom or in the entrance to a field, with his wheeled dustbin on hand, and on such occasions I would stop for a chat. In time I realized that these occasions were his official breaks. He started work at 7.30, with a ten-minute ''lowance' break mid-morning, a dinner break of half an hour at noon and a tea break of ten minutes during the afternoon, before finishing at 4.30 p.m. When I realized that these were his break time, I avoided chatting to him then – after all, a man is entitled to some time free from the cares of office – and I tried to talk to him when he was actually on his feet and going about his daily routine. He did not mind such interruptions, but I felt he should have some privacy. My own job had taught me the value of a meal which is uninterrupted by public demands.

Through regularly patrolling those self-same lanes, I became accustomed to Rodney's break times. I began to realize that when he was sweeping the grit of winter from the roads, to gather it and replace it in nice heaps by the roadside, he would take his first break at 10 a.m., with dinner at noon and his tea break at 2.30 p.m., all being serviced from the flasks, sandwiches, cakes and fruit he carried with him.

Then one bright and sunny June morning, at 9.30 a.m., I noticed him sitting in the entrance to a field just beyond Crampton Lane End. It was a junction where the lane from Crampton emerged onto the busier Malton to Ashfordly road. The road sloped quite steeply down to that junction, and Rodney's chosen gateway was right on the corner. It gave him long views along the road and up the hill. I could see him for some time before I arrived. His bin was nearby as usual, but this was half an hour earlier than his normal time and, knowing Rodney's meticulous time-keeping, I wondered if something was wrong. Maybe he was ill?

I drew up and parked, then clambered out to meet him.

'Morning, Rodney,' I greeted him. 'All right?'

'Aye, Mr Rhea.' He was munching a piece of fruitcake and had a flask of coffee at his side. 'It's 'lowance time.'

'You're early,' I said. 'I thought you might be ill.'

'Nay, Ah'm fine. They've changed my times.'

I presumed 'they' were the council.

'Oh, well, I won't trouble you . . .'

'We've changed areas,' he added, as if in explanation. 'Ah was under Ashfordly, now Ah'm under Brantsford, so they've changed my 'lowance time. Half-nine instead of ten.'

'But does it really matter?' I asked in all innocence.

'Aye, well, if they say half-nine, then half-nine it is. Ah mean, it *is* a bit early, if you ask me, but, well, Ah'm not in a position to argue.'

'No,' I smiled. 'We must all do as we're told, Rodney. Well, I must be off. I'm meeting the sergeant at Ashfordly, and I'd better not keep him waiting.'

'It's a nuisance, all this chopping and changing,' he grumbled as I prepared to leave. 'Ah can't see why they must keep on changing. Progress is all right so long as it doesn't change anything. That's how Ah sees it.'

I could sympathize with him. I have a theory that council managers and their white-collar staff, including their counterparts in other public bodies, regularly reorganize things in order to keep themselves in a job. Much work is generated by any reorganization, and at times it means that more staff are recruited to cope with the increase in paperwork. Reorganizations are wonderful job-creation schemes, even if they never achieve an improvement in efficiency or cost.

'You'll be on half-nine 'lowance for a while then?'

'Aye,' he said. 'And here, for all this week. I'm on this length, cutting hedges, trimming verges, guttering and the like.'

'I'll see you around then!' I smiled and drove away.

Sure enough, for the next couple of days, he was sitting in that same gateway from precisely 9.30 a.m. until 9.40 a.m.

And then, on the Thursday, I had an awful shock. I was on an early patrol, having started at 6 a.m., and my own breakfast break was scheduled for 10 a.m. at my own police house in Aidensfield. But a few minutes after 9.30 a.m. I received a radio call from Control to the effect that a lorry had run off the road and had gone through the hedge into a field at Crampton Lane End. There were injuries; an ambulance had been called, and a man who lived in a cottage at the lane end had witnessed the accident. He'd called the police with the news that somebody had been hurt. There were no further details. Switching on my blue light, I dashed to the scene. As I approached, I found myself worrying about Rodney. He had his break at Crampton Lane End at half past nine, and I knew the gateway was directly in the line of a runaway lorry . . . I pressed the accelerator.

I was relieved when I could not see his wheeled dustbin, but as I parked and hurried to the crashed lorry, I realized it had run away down the hill, over the verge and then through the very gateway that Rodney occupied. And it must have gone through as near 9.30 a.m. as made no difference. So where was he?

The lorry had run into the field beyond, then nose-dived into a hollow; its load of rubble had not shifted, but the driver was trapped in his cab. I found him groaning in agony; his leg appeared to be trapped somewhere near the foot pedals. He was alone. Jim Lewis from the cottage was on hand and helped me give comfort to the driver. I radioed for the fire brigade, saying we would need cutting gear, and in the busy time which followed, I forgot about Rodney. He was nowhere to be seen. In time, we released the driver and rushed him off to hospital with a suspected broken leg, chest injuries and concussion, then a breakdown truck was contacted to remove the damaged lorry.

I now had an accident report to compile, and my day would be fully occupied. I gave no further thought to Rodney's near-brush with death until I had to fill in the accident report later that day. I was working in the office which is attached to the police house, using my faithful little typewriter. In the space for 'Time of Accident', I wrote '9.30 a.m.', the time given to me by Jim Lewis. He was sure about that – he'd tuned into the radio news just as the lorry crashed. As I entered the time, I wondered where Rodney had got to. But even as I worked, there was a knock on the office door. I opened it to find Rodney standing there, accompanied by his faithful bin.

'Oh, hello, Rodney. Come in.'

'Nay, Ah shan't stay, Mr Rhea. Ah just wondered if Ah could ask a favour.'

'Of course. What is it?'

'That wagon this morning, it went through yon gateway . . .'

'And I was very worried that you could have been injured,' I said. 'It went right through that gate you've been using – and spot on half past nine too!'

'Aye, Ah know, but, you see, Mr Rhea, Ah didn't have my 'lowance till ten this morning. I wasn't there when she crashed.'

'You could have been killed if you had been there!' I cried.

'Aye, t'reason Ah came was, well, if anybody from t'council asks, Ah'd not want 'em to know Ah took my 'lowance break late.'

'I can't imagine anybody checking on that, Rodney!'

'Well, you never can tell, Mr Rhea. Ah mean, Ah'm supposed to take 'lowance at half-nine, not ten. And today Ah didn't. Ah took it late, you see . . . contrary to instructions.'

'And saved your own life in the process, eh?' I smiled.

'But you will back me up, won't you?'

'Of course I will, Rodney. If anybody asks, I'll say you were in that next gateway, eh? At half past nine.'

'Aye,' he relaxed now. 'Thanks, Ah'll say t' same.'

'As a matter of interest, Rodney, why did you take a late 'lowance?'

'My old cart got a flat tyre. I took her to t'garage to get it fixed and took my 'lowance there, while they fixed it. It took me half an hour to get there, you see . . .'

'I see,' I smiled. 'Never fear, Rodney, your secret is safe with me.'

And off he went, very pleased at his own piece of subterfuge. I don't think he realized he owed his life to that flat tyre, but I did wonder what went through his mind each day as he worried about his unseen bosses. If I knew them, they wouldn't know of his existence. Poor old Rodney, he was a slave to his own conscience, a lovely chap.

3 *'Sup That!'*

> Mid pleasures and palaces though we may roam,
> Be it ever so humble, there's no place like home.
>
> J.H. Payne (1791-1852)

One aspect of rural life which continues to fascinate me is the wealth of differing styles in the cottages and houses found in most small villages. In some cases, they are in very isolated locations. They represent the entire range of social classes and aspirations, but in a village community most of their owners live happily together. Millionaires and professional people live next door to labourers and lorry-drivers. You cannot reproduce that social mix in modern housing estates – they tend to be limited to people of one kind or class, and the houses are all too similar.

Most of us know of stockbrokers' ghettos, professional parades, executive avenues and council towerblocks, but these communities lack the character of a true village whose community spirit has matured over centuries. I believe that in modern times no one is capable of designing or constructing a genuine village with all its charm, benefits and close-knit atmosphere. A village needs time to mature; it must evolve over many generations and contain many generations. A true village is a splendid place in which to live and bring up one's children.

So far as the houses are concerned, the lack of planning control in times past has produced a fascinating mixture of good and bad, of ugly and beautiful, of large and small. At one end of the scale, there is the grandeur of the Big House where His Lordship or the squire used to live (and in many cases continues to live), and at the other there is the rustic simplicity of tiny cottages which serve the basic needs of their occupants. Between these extremes is a range of other homes, sometimes in terraces, sometimes semi-detached, but very frequently standing alone in a much-loved piece of well-tended ground. All are rich in contrast and full of interest.

Perhaps that is over-simplifying the position, especially as it affects the moorland and dales around Aidensfield. For example, the word 'hall' can indicate something as massive as Castle Howard, which achieved fame as 'Brideshead' on television, or it could refer to a small farm deep in the hills. One famous hall on the edge of my beat had a cricket field on the lawn where the Yorkshire first team would sometimes play. In direct contrast, I have visited halls which were smaller than a semi-detached house.

Similarly, the name 'castle' appears in the names of some houses. Danby Castle in Eskdale is a small working farm, although in Henry VIII's time it *was* a castle. Indeed, one of his wives, Catherine Parr, lived here. There are other occupied homes around the moors which bear the suffix 'castle' and are very handsome and well-maintained; these are not open to the public because they are private houses. Of several Bumper Castles, one is a farm, while another is a pub. Slingsby Castle, for example, is not a true castle. It is a fine example of an Elizabethan type of house, although it dates from the time of Charles II. Now in ruins, it was never completed and has never been occupied – but it is massive and imposing, even though it was built for a dwarf, Sir Charles Cavendish. He was clearly a little man with big ideas.

Contradictions can also be found in the word 'house'. A dwelling with this common name can be very substantial or it might be a tiny cottage nestling in the quieter part of a moorland village. For the patrolling constable, it all means that one cannot gain a true impression of a person's home merely from its name.

One example was Bracken Hill Farm at Gelderslack. Believing its name has some rapport with the moors, I expected a small hill farm of the kind that had survived for generations, but to my surprise I found a massive spread of whitewashed buildings, with a hacienda that might have come from Spain, a range of satellite extensions that reminded me of a Californian ranch, and views that reminded me of the Loire Valley in France. Even the vehicles in the farmyard might have come from either Texas or the Motor Show.

Another surprise occurred when I was called by a lady who looked after Meadow Cottage, Crampton, while its owners were away.

As I motored to the address, I sought a pretty cottage sitting on the edge of a field replete with colourful wild flowers. Instead, I found a massive establishment with a courtyard surrounded by stables and looseboxes, complete with fabulous gardens overlooked by a house that occupied the space of half a dozen semi-detached dwellings. The gardens were spread along the banks of the river, and a small boat was moored at the edge of the lawn. It was probably the most unlikely 'cottage' I have ever encountered.

The reason for the lady's call is worthy of inclusion. She was housekeeper to Mr and Mrs Rudolph Faulkner. He was a top executive for a Yorkshire brewing company and was regularly away on business, often overseas. His wife, Felicity, sometimes accompanied him, and this was such an occasion. They had left the housekeeper, Mrs Winnie Hilton, in charge of their home for a couple of weeks. Winnie lived nearby and was the widow of a retired farmworker.

Just before lunch one Sunday, as she gazed across her garden fence, she noticed two coaches halt outside Meadow Cottage. This was not unusual, for the village did attract tourists. On this occasion, she watched a gaggle of almost a hundred people climb out. It was a warm, sunny day in June, and they were all armed with picnic equipment. At this point Winnie became horrified, because they all trooped through the gates of the Faulkners' home and into the splendid gardens before ambling across the lawns towards the river bank. Each was seeking a good place to enjoy a picnic. In this part of the country, it is a sad fact that some dopey visitors do wander into private gardens, but this was a mass invasion. Surely they had not mistaken Meadow Cottage for Castle Howard or Crampton Hall?

Winnie rushed outside to remonstrate with the bus-drivers, but they replied that they had been told to stop here for a picnic lunch. They had no idea who had given the orders to their firm; their order had come from their head office. She knew that if such a visit had been sanctioned by the Faulkners, she would have been informed. In the absence of such consent, she rang me to complain about the trespassers.

I was in the middle of my lunch and, as this was not an emergency, I spent another five minutes finishing my meal before driving the few miles to Crampton. This pretty village stands on the banks of the River Rye and is a delight; it is virtually unspoilt and presents a continuing aura of rustic calm. But things were not very calm that day because Winnie was stalking up and down in her pinny, her face as black as thunder.

'Now, Winnie,' I said, 'what's this all about?'

She repeated her story, pointing to the hordes of people on the Faulkners' lawn. They were enjoying their meal, for it was a splendid situation.

For my part, I knew my official limitations so far as trespass was concerned – simple trespass is not a criminal offence, nor is it a police matter. It could enter the realms of criminal law if certain other factors were incorporated, such as the pursuit of game or when committing malicious damage. But if these people did not have the Faulkners' authority, I felt I should at least try to remove them. I might be justified in so doing on the grounds that I was preventing a breach of the peace by Winnie!

As she fussed and grumbled, I spoke to the bus-drivers, who said they were simply obeying orders, and I then asked who was in charge of the party. They said it was a Mr Williamson, who was among the crowd by the river. With Winnie at my side, I set about locating him. My uniformed arrival caused something of a stir as I marched around and called for Mr Williamson. Eventually a nervous-looking individual with thin, light hair and rimmed spectacles disentangled himself from the crowd. In his early forties, he wore a green blazer and lighter green trousers, and I saw that most of the others in the party wore the same uniform. I now realized that the party comprised adults and young people mainly in their late teens. He faced me with a show of bravery and said, 'I'm Stanley Williamson.'

After introducing myself, I explained the problem as I understood it, but he looked puzzled.

'No, Mr Rhea, we have permission, I assure you. I got it from the headmaster.'

'But it's not his house. He can't give permission.' I pointed out. 'The Faulkners are away, and I'm assured they have not agreed to this.'

'They'd 'ave told me,' chipped in Winnie Hilton at my side.

My chat with Mr Williamson revealed that this was a party of choristers and musicians from a Yorkshire public school. They were on their way to give a concert at Keldford Hall, which lay about an hour's drive beyond Crampton. They were due there around 2.30 p.m. for rehearsals, and the concert was to begin at 6.30 p.m. after an early evening meal. The headmaster had suggested a break on the journey, hence the picnic lunch in the grounds of Meadow Cottage.

''E once came to stay here,' announced Winnie.

'Who did?' I asked her.

'That headmaster. He came for a weekend.'

'So he knows the house and the Faulkners?'

'Aye,' she said. 'Tim's at school there.'

I now began to see the proverbial dim light at the end of the proverbial long tunnel. 'Tim?' I asked.

'Their son, Timothy, 'e's in the sixth form.'

'That's right,' chipped in Mr Williamson. 'He should have been here today, he plays the violin, but he couldn't make it. He's broken his finger, playing cricket . . .'

'I think we'd better have words with the headmaster,' I suggested. 'Can we do it from the house?' I put to Winnie.

With Williamson and Winnie at my side, I entered the splendid lounge, courtesy of Winnie's key, and rang the school. Since it was a boarding school, the headmaster was available.

Upon my explaining the problem, he told me that when this concert had been first proposed, several months ago, he had asked Timothy Faulkner whether it would be agreeable if the choristers and orchestra halted at his parents' house. Knowing the house and its grounds, the head felt it was the ideal point for a break in the long journey. Tim had said it would be fine. The head had expected him to clear this proposal with his parents – clearly, Tim had not bothered.

To give due credit to the headmaster, two or three days before finalizing his arrangements he had called Tim to his study to check that his parents had approved the proposal. Tim, not admitting he had forgotten to ask and wishing to keep faith with the head, and also knowing that his parents would be out of the country on the day, had confirmed the plans.

'Obviously, Mr Rhea, there has been a breakdown in communication,' he said, and I could sense his embarrassment.

'So I've got a hundred trespassers in the grounds of an empty house,' I told him and, with him still on the line, I relayed the explanation to Winnie.

'That's just t'sort o' trick young Mr Tim would do,' she sighed. ''E really is the limit . . .'

'Can I suggest we allow these people to remain, provided they leave no mess?' I put to her.

'Aye,' she nodded. 'Seeing Mr Tim's said so.'

And so the crisis was over.

As Winnie locked the house, I walked away with Mr Williamson, who said, 'Thanks for sorting that out, Mr Rhea. The lady was upset.'

'She was just doing her job – and so was I. So you go back and enjoy the picnic – but please make sure your people leave things tidy, eh?'

'I will – and, look, by way of apologizing for the trouble we've caused, I've two complimentary tickets,' he dug into his pocket. 'Maybe you and Mrs Rhea would like to join us?'

'I'd love to,' I said. 'But how about Winnie and a friend? She's had more hassle than me! She has no transport, so it would mean taking her with you on one of these buses and then bringing her back again.'

'I think, under the circumstances, we could fix that,' he smiled.

And so Winnie Hilton and her friend Alice saw the rehearsals, had a meal with the group and had a look around Keldford Hall before going to the concert.

'By gum, Mr Rhea,' she said when I saw her a few days later in the village, 'I did enjoy yon concert. It's t'first time I've been to a posh affair like that.'

'What about Mr Faulkner? Was he upset about those picnickers?' I asked eventually.

'I never told him,' she said slyly. And neither did I.

Because the Faulkners' cottage was so splendid, I expected a similar spread at Thorngill Grange, a dwelling high on the moors above Gelderslack.

The reason for my call involved a missing hiker. A middle-aged man called Simon Milner had decided to tackle the long-distance Blackamoor Walk and had not arrived home at the expected time. He had been due back at tea time the day before my enquiries. Sensibly, Mr Milner junior had allowed time for his father to turn up or make contact before raising the alarm, but as neither had happened by breakfast time next morning, he decided to inform us.

Sergeant Charlie Bairstow took the call when I was in the office at Ashfordly.

'Right, Mr Milner, we'll circulate a description – I don't intend instituting a full search just yet. Perhaps he's called at a pub somewhere and stayed overnight?'

'A pub!' Milner junior had apparently been horrified at the suggestion. 'My father does not go into public houses, Sergeant. He is a Methodist lay preacher . . . a teetotaller . . . a man of strong principles and high morals!'

'It's just a thought, Mr Milner. No offence meant. I mean, our moorland inns are havens of refuge, you know, not dens of iniquity. You'll be sure to call us if he does turn up?'

He said he would keep us informed.

We circulated a physical description of the hiker, but at this early stage there was no real cause for alarm. Mr Milner, in his middle fifties, was an experienced rambler and was not known to be suffering from any illness or disease. Searching for hikers who had become overdue was a regular feature of our work. Many simply strayed from their chosen path or took longer than they had planned; more often than not, they found temporary accommodation in barns, inns and boarding houses, or even in friendly farms and cottages. In the case of Mr Milner, however, it seemed we could ignore the hospitality of the moorland inns.

Sadly, some hikers are a nuisance. Those who walk alone seldom bother to tell anyone of their route or intention, nor do they advise us of any enforced delay. As a consequence, at the behest of anxious friends or relatives, we often find ourselves searching for them, albeit in a very perfunctory manner in the early stages. But if they do not turn up, genuine concern develops and the longer the delay, the greater the concern and the more intensified the search, But, realistically, where does one begin to search 553 square miles of elevated and open moorland?

It was a curious fact that, in the months before Mr Milner's case, we had experienced an increasing number of problems with hikers. This had been especially noticeable among those attempting the long-distance Blackamoor Walk, a trek of around seventy miles across the loftier parts of the moors. It had become quite commonplace for some to stroll into Ashfordly market-place in the early hours of the morning, singing and shouting, having consumed bottles of strong liquor along their way. In some cases, there was a definite party atmosphere, and it seemed that parties of hikers were making whoopee somewhere on the hills. Their overdue return to civilization had not seemed to bother them, even if it had created anxiety among their friends and families.

As there were no pubs on the actual route of the Walk, these people must have diverted a considerable distance to get supplies – and that would cause delays and ultimately some worries among loved-ones waiting at home or at check-points. But there was another problem – in their happiness at reaching civilization, their singing and exuberance awoke the residents of Ashfordly; furthermore, they left their litter all over the place and in many cases became noisy, unpleasant and unwanted. It is fair to add that some who became too abusive or obnoxious ended their trip in our cells and even in court.

Some would sleep off the booze in barns or even in the open fields, but even in these cases, anyone who was overdue was likely to become the focus of an expensive search by the police or Moorland Rescue Search Party. Clearly, the upright and sober Mr Milner was not in this category. I could not imagine him rolling home in full voice after a session in a moorland pub.

It was ten o'clock that morning when I left Ashfordly police station to resume my patrol, and in the absence of more urgent work I decided to carry out a limited search for Mr Milner. I selected the area around Thorngill Grange. In that vicinity, a section of the Blackamoor Walk passed through the north-western corner of my beat before terminating at Ashfordly.

Having determined that Mr Milner was expected to conclude his hike along this stretch, I decided upon a modest search of the surrounding moor. A check on the map showed that Thorngill Grange stood on the edge of the heathered heights, close to where the Walk dipped from the more remote sections before entering a wooded glen for its final three miles or so. Until now, I had never had any reason to visit Thorngill Grange, but a check on the Electoral Register showed me that it was occupied by Albert and Dorothy Potter. I had no more information about the place or its inhabitants.

It did not take long to discover that it was even more remote than the map had suggested. I reached the end of a rough, unmade track some time before catching sight of the house. The track deteriorated into a primitive footpath across the heather before dropping into the dale beyond. When I parked at the brow of the ridge, I could see the house sitting at the head of the dale. It would require a considerable hike to reach it. But this was neither a mansion, a gentleman's residence nor even a farm. It was a tiny thatched cottage, one end of which was derelict while the other seemed barely suitable for anyone to occupy. A dry stone wall surrounded the cottage, but there was no name on the small wooden gate which opened into the paddock and nothing to indicate that this was Thorngill Grange. There was no other building nearby. The house stood utterly alone.

Beyond, on the heights above the other side of this tiny dale, was the open moor, treeless, flat and awe-inspiring. The wild expanse of heather was within a few days of bursting into the gorgeous purple which is so beautiful and dramatic. Running from the heights was a moorland stream, the Thorn Gill which gave its name to this cottage, and it flowed down a narrow cleft in the hills, eventually to reach the River Rye near Rievaulx Abbey. Black-faced sheep roamed these moors without the benefit of fencing, and the paths they had created over the centuries criss-crossed among the heather, some being utilized by an increasing number of ramblers and hikers.

The Blackamoor Walk traversed these high and lonely moors, and indeed there was a primitive stone footbridge across the gill. It led from the main route of the Walk towards Thorngill Grange, and I guessed the Potters made use of it to check their sheep and lambs if indeed they farmed the moor. But the bridge was not part of the Walk – the route passed the end of it.

The views from this point were staggering in their range and beauty, and as a perfect hideaway, Thorngill Grange must surely be a dream. Perhaps the Potters used it only as a country cottage? I would soon know the answer.

I opened the gate, which squeaked a little, and was greeted by a black-and-white Border collie who fussed around my legs as I made for the unpainted oak door. It opened even before I reached it, and a very short, very fat woman in her late sixties stood before me. Her greying hair was pulled back in a tight bun, and she was wiping her hands on her apron; they were covered in flour, I noted.

'By gum,' she smiled through gums which contained about a third of their complement of teeth, 'it's a policeman!'

'Hello,' I greeted her. 'I'm PC Rhea from Aidensfield.'

'Well then, you'd better come in and sit down. Ah've a kettle on t'hob. You'll have a cup o' tea and a bun?'

This was not an invitation – it was a statement of fact, because it was customary for the moorland folk to entertain visitors in this way, and I had arrived at ''lowance time'.

I ducked under the low beam above the doorway, the straw thatching brushing my head as I removed my cap, and found myself stepping back a century or even further. The low roof was heavily beamed in dark oak. Some polished horse brasses, genuine ones, plus a few horseshoes, were crudely nailed to some cross timbers. The floor was of smooth sandstone, and it bore a clip rug before the fireplace. The fireplace was a massive hole in the thick stone wall; in the right of the gap was a black oven with a brass handle and an ornate design on the door, while to the right was the hot water boiler, identified by the tap under which was a ladling can, a white enamel mug with a handle; it caught the drips from the tap. A peat fire was smouldering between them, and above it was a smoke hood, a relic of bygone times. Above the smouldering peat, hanging on a large hook which in turn dangled from an adjustable rail, was a large black kettle. It was singing all the time. In spite of the bright sunshine outside, the room was dark and cool.

Before asking the purpose of my visit, the little fat lady busied herself with warming the tea-pot, then disappeared into the pantry, where she piled a plate full of cakes, buns and cheese. She set it all before me on the plain, scrubbed wooden table, one end of which she was utilizing for her baking. She produced some milk in a metal can and poured it into a mug. Only then did she pour the water onto the tea leaves, and as the tea brewed, she continued with her baking as she talked to me. She was in fact making a 'tatie and onion pie, which she thrust into the oven. Then she settled beside me.

'That's for his dinner. Now then, what can I do for you?' Her smile revealed those awful gaps in her teeth. 'It's nice to 'ave a visitor, Mr Rhea.'

'Are you Mrs Potter?' I asked.

'Aye, that's me. Our Albert's out at work. Was it him you wanted?'

'Not particularly,' I answered, and then explained the purpose of my call, giving her a brief description of the missing Mr Milner. She listened, nodding from time to time.

'Aye, a chap like yon did pop in last night. He was fit and well, and we sent him on his way. They do come wandering this way,' she said slowly. 'They see yon bridge over t'gill and think it's part of t'main route. Some are that tired, they're walking in their sleep and just need an hour or two's rest. Ah've slept 'em in 'ere on bad nights, but yon middle-aged feller didn't stay. We gave him a drink and off he went. Singing tiv himself, he was. 'The Old Rugged Cross', I reckon it was supposed to be. He was in good fettle, Mr Rhea, I'll say that, and said he was heading for Ashfordly.'

'Thanks. I can check further down the dale. But if he does come back, ask him to get in touch with his son or the police at Ashfordly. He's overdue and we are just a bit worried about him.'

'Some daft folks treat these moors as if they're parks and gardens,' she said. 'They need respect, these moors, eh?'

'They do,' I agreed, and now she was pouring my mug of tea. She pushed the plate of cakes towards me.

I stayed longer than I should have, for she provided me with a fascinating account of her life at this remote place.

Her husband, Albert, had once farmed this patch of land, rearing sheep and Highland cattle, but as he was now nearing sixty-five, with no pension in sight, he had turned his hand to freelance gardening. This morning he was working for Sir William Ashdale and would be home for his dinner just after twelve. I decided to stay and meet him, for it was now almost twelve, and besides, that pie smelt wonderful . . .

Mrs Potter showed me around the little house, which they owned – they had paid £120 for it a few years earlier. The derelict portion had turf walls, parts of which were still standing, while its roof, once thatched with heather, had collapsed. There had been no attempt to repair it. That was where Albert had once kept his cattle or shorn his sheep. A cross passage separated that part from the living-accommodation, all of which was on the ground floor. There were two tiny bedrooms, each with a stone floor and beamed ceiling, but no bathroom or running water. They obtained their water from the gill; the toilet was a shed behind the cottage, and for electricity they had installed a generator which was petrol-driven – that was their only modern contraption.

By the time this tour ended, Albert had arrived. He used a pedal cycle of considerable size and vintage. His shovel, rake, hoe and gripe were tied to the crossbar. He placed his bike in a shed, then came towards me.

'Now then,' he said in the local manner of greeting.

'Now then.' I shook his hand. 'I'm PC Rhea.'

'Albert Potter,' he introduced himself. 'Thoo'll be coming in for thi dinner then?'

'No thanks. I had my 'lowance here not long since.'

'But it's dinner time now, and Ah shall be having mine, so you might as well join me.'

And so I did; I was not expected to refuse.

He was a tall and lanky fellow with arms and legs that seemed too long for his thin body. He wore a thick blue-and-white striped shirt with the sleeves rolled up, but with no collar. The neck was open, and a collar stud occupied one of the buttonholes. Heavy brown boots and thick brown trousers with braces completed his outfit. Fit and bronzed, he looked remarkably strong for a man in his middle sixties, but he was a man of few words. He sat and ate in silence, and I did likewise, savouring the potato and onion pie, then the apple pie and custard that followed. Then, without speaking, he went to a cupboard and opened it to reveal shelves full of bottles without labels. They contained fluids – red, yellow, brown, dark brown, dark blue, orange and other variations. He selected one which was full of a purplish liquid, removed the cork with a corkscrew, then poured me a glass full.

'Sup that,' he said. 'It'll put hairs on your chest.'

'What is it?' I asked, tentatively sniffing at the potion.

'Bilberry wine, good stuff. Eight years old if it's a day. Our Dot makes it,' and he drank deeply.

Wary of the fact that I was on duty and that I had to drive back, I took a sip. It was lethal. I had but a thimbleful and even with that tiny amount could sense its power – but it was really beautiful, smooth and full, rich with the flavour of the moors. But for all its beauty and delectability, it was powerful stuff.

'Good year for bilberries that year,' he said. 'Have some more, lad. See whether you can tell me whether them berries came from Sutton Bank Top or Bransdale or Fryup Dale.'

'You mean they all taste different?'

'They do that! Once you know 'em, they're as easy to tell apart as French grapes.'

I tried a little more, hoping for some indication of its source . . .

Weakening, I tried still more, encouraged by this sombre character.

'I think it's Bransdale,' I said, but in truth I had no idea.

'No, this 'un's Bransdale,' and he produced another bottle from somewhere. 'Now, just you see t'difference.'

'I shouldn't,' I said. 'I mean, I am on duty . . .'

'Rubbish, it's good for your arteries, cleans 'em out, gets rid o' clots . . . here.'

He poured a huge helping and, in order to satisfy myself that there was a difference between Sutton Bank bilberries and Bransdale bilberries, I took a sip. Then I took a little more, just to make sure I was receiving the full flavour.

As I was doing my best to identify any distinctions, Dorothy came in.

'There's a couple of hikers at the door,' she said to her husband. 'They're asking for two bottles of Rievaulx rhubarb, two Ashfordly elderberry, two Egton Bridge gooseberry, two Rannockdale raspberry and a couple of Bransdale bramble.'

'There's enough, I reckon,' said Albert.

And as I became aware that I was slightly fuddled by the strong liquor, he poured me another helping, saying this was Fryup bilberries and maybe I'd like to compare it with the Fryup brambles or perhaps the Hollin Wood sloes. I was vaguely aware of Mrs Potter returning to put some money in a tin and of her husband saying, 'Think on and fetch a few bottles up from t'cellar. Dot . . .'

'Er,' – I sensed that my brain was no longer operating my voice in an efficient constabulary manner, but hoped I did not sound too stupid. 'Er, Albert, when that man called last night, the hiker we're looking for, er, well, did he sample your wine?'

'Aye,' said Albert. 'He said he never drank alcohol, so Ah said this wasn't alcohol. Ah told him it was home-made wine, full o' fruit and flavour. So he had a few, and that made him happier, so he bought a few bottles before he set off. Six, I think; all he could fit in his rucksack. He reckoned our Bilsdale bramble was like nectar and couldn't get enough of the Hambleton haw wine.'

'I'd better go for a walk,' I said, rising somewhat uncertainly from the chair.

'It's worst when you've had nowt to eat,' said Albert. 'But give it an hour and you'll be as right as rain.'

I thanked them, and they presented me with a bottle of Byland potato and Ashfordly redcurrant, which I placed in the van. The radio was burbling but I could not decipher the words – it wouldn't be a message for me. With legs feeling distinctly wobbly, I set off towards that little stone bridge; I could see two or three little stone bridges, so I aimed for the middle one, doused my head in the cool waters of that gill and then walked briskly in the fresh air. I walked for a long time, blissfully unaware of the hours that passed, but I did find a barn.

Quite suddenly, as Albert had indicated, I felt fine. It was almost as if a miracle had happened: the fuzziness cleared like a fog lifting, and I was sure I was no longer under the influence of Potter wine. I realized that the barn offered sanctuary for hikers – or constables who were sweating profusely and perhaps, if the truth was admitted, still just a little unsteady on their feet. And there, in the cool of the afternoon, I found the missing Mr Simon Milner. He was sitting on a bale of hay, singing softly to himself, with two empty bottles at his side.

'Mr Milner?' I managed to say.

'After goodnoon, Oshiffer.' He made a clumsy attempt at saluting me. 'I say, you should neck this sampler . . . sample this nectar . . . er . . . dog of the drigs . . . drink of the gods . . . God is a funderful wellow, eh? Giving us the earths of the fruit . . . providing us with the greed . . . the . . . ingredients . . .'

By now, I was reasonably in command of my own senses. 'Come along, Mr Milner, it's time to go home.'

He started to sing 'Time to go home' in the manner of television's Andy Pandy programme and waved his hand like that little puppet. I wished his son could see him now. With something of a struggle, I managed to get him back to the van and plonked him in the passenger seat.

I decided to tell Mr and Mrs Potter that I'd found him. As I went to their door, four more hikers were leaving with bottles of the potent Potter potion, and I now knew why we had so many very merry and excitable hikers in Ashfordly. They had no need of a pub with a supply of this kind available.

I thanked the Potters for their hospitality and left, driving Mr Milner down to the youth hostel in case his son had alerted them. As I drove away, I heard the radio calling me – and with horror I realized I had been off the air and out of contact for hours. The sergeant knew I was heading for the heights, and in all probability their inability to contact me since eleven that morning would mean I had been posted lost on the moors . . .

'Echo Seven,' called Control in a voice that rang with exasperation and worry. 'Echo Seven, receiving? Over.'

'Echo Seven receiving,' I responded in what I hoped was a matter-of-fact, calm manner. My head was clear. I was horrified to see it was nearly 4.30!

There was a long silence, and then another voice said, 'Echo Seven. Location please.'

'Echo Seven, Thorngill Moor, near the Blackamoor Walk route. I have just located the missing man, Mr Simon Milner. He is with me in the vehicle; he is fit and well, no injuries. My intended destination is Ashfordly youth hostel. Over.'

I could explain my long absence by saying I had obtained several differing clues and conflicting sightings about the hiker's whereabouts and, due to the uncertainty, it had taken me several hours to locate my quarry. The fact that I had found him would undoubtedly save me from a mammoth bollocking.

'Echo Seven. Upon your return, report to the duty inspector. He wishes to give you advice. A search party has been organized to look for you – you never booked off the air and there has been great concern . . .

I groaned as Control gave me a well-deserved reprimand over the air. I knew I had been guilty of the self-same thoughtlessness as the many hikers and, like them, I had imbibed the powerful juices of the Potters. I did not try to excuse myself over the radio, but sighed as I turned for home.

Mr Milner sighed at my side, but he was asleep; he was now in his own world of bucolic and alcoholic bliss; a nice story for his chapel friends when he recovered. But I suppose he could be honest because, after all, even though he had strayed from his ways like a lost sheep, he had not entered a pub.

As I drove through acres of maturing heather, a very official thought occurred to me. If the Potters were selling intoxicating liquor, they would require a justices' licence and an excise licence, and they would have to abide by the licensing hours. Or would they need an off-licence, seeing their customers did not drink inside the premises? If customers did enter to drink, the premises could be classified as public house, and in addition there were certain requirements applicable to the brewing of wines and spirits . . .

I groaned. It all threatened to become very complicated.

I felt that a word of warning about the laws of selling intoxicants would be my first task, rather than a heavy-handed prosecution which involved the Customs and Excise and the Liquor Licensing laws. But I did not know whether I dare return, because if I did, old Albert would probably ask me to test his Rannockdale turnip, Lairsbeck parsnip or Thackerston carrot. I wasn't sure I would be able to resist.

I decided it might be best to overlook this particular episode, due to my own involuntary involvement and, to be precise, I had no direct proof of their sale to customers. Hints yes, but not proof.

But I could not shirk my duty. I decided that I must return to advise Dot and Albert on the illegality of selling their wine, if only to give Ashfordly and its people a break from merry ramblers.

I did learn afterwards that news of this establishment had reached the rambling clubs that passed this way and that most of their members made a point of calling for refreshment. Perhaps if the Potters opened a licensed restaurant, they would be able to make some money? I might put that idea to them.

Because they were not at that time licensed, it did mean that Mr Milner had not disgraced himself by frequenting a pub. But right now I had to get Mr Milner home and prepare myself for a telling-off by the inspector.

'Come on, Mr Milner,' I said to the inert figure in my passenger seat. 'It's time to go home . . .'

'Time to go home, time to go home.' In his fuddled state, he started to sing and wave ta-ta.

4 *April Fool!*

A joke's a very serious thing.
Charles Churchill (1731–64)

When our eldest child, Elizabeth, started at the village school, we felt sure she would quickly learn all that was necessary to equip her for the future. Each afternoon, we would ask what she had learned that day, and it seemed that she was progressing very satisfactorily. Then one day she announced she had learned about April Fool jokes. I could not ascertain whether this gem of wisdom had come from the teachers or her classmates, but with the solemnity that only a 5-year-old can muster, she did say that the jokes must end at noon on 1 April and that nobody must be hurt by the pranks. This suggested a sense of responsibility.

Because this fruitful portion of learning had come to my notice in mid-March, I had forgotten about it by 1 April. Like almost everyone else, though, I was aware of April Fool jokes – indeed, police officers throughout the country play jokes upon each other or their bosses, taking care never to harm or disrupt the public peace in so doing. I have recounted several of these in earlier *Constable* books (see *Constable through the Meadow*).

For example, one mild joke involved an alteration of a list of telephone numbers in the police station – the superintendent's private number was listed as the 'new' number for the speaking clock. When an unsuspecting constable checked the time at 3 a.m., his enquiry was not well received.

Another constable had his private car number placed on the stolen vehicle index and as a result got stopped countless times by officers of other forces while on his way to a fishing match. Some constables have been told to check mortuaries for security, only to see 'corpses' sit up in the darkness. Another was confronted by a road-sweeper who was cleaning the town's street at 3 a.m. This rookie constable, having been told to stop and interview all suspicious people seen around at night, spoke to this character. The sweeper said he liked cleaning the streets at this time of day because it was quiet and they didn't get messed up again before he finished. In fact, the heavily disguised road-sweeper was one of his colleagues whom, as he was new to the town, the rookie did not recognize.

I have been guilty of some jokes too, several of which have appeared in print, such as the reported discovery of a gold mine in the grounds of Coultersdale Abbey, a North Yorkshire ruin, the appearance of the legendary boves in England from which we get the saying 'Heaven's a bove', and the location of a colony of miniature blind sabre-toothed tigers in an ancient Yorkshire caving system.

In addition to these pranks, there have been offers of lead-free pencils, UFO sightings, cars with self-repairing punctures, and the stone-by-stone removal of Whitby Abbey to a new site.

I liked John Blashford-Snell's account of a tribe of natives who carried their heads under their arms, and Richard Dimbleby's famous television documentary about the spaghetti harvest. And there are many others that have appealed to my sense of humour.

But I did not like 5-year-old Elizabeth's April Fool joke.

It began one Saturday morning, when she was off school. She was out of bed rather early, and I should have expected something of a mischievous nature from the knowing grin on her face. But, like a lamb going to slaughter, the significance of the date had temporarily escaped me as I concentrated on lots of paperwork which I had to complete before going on duty. I ignored the danger signs exhibited by Elizabeth, one of which involved her hanging around my office while looking distinctly pleased with herself.

I was working mornings, which was especially pleasing on a Saturday, and I now had a four-hour route to perform. This had been pre-determined by the sergeant. I had to begin at 9 a.m., patrol to Elsinby for a 10 a.m. point at the telephone kiosk, followed by points at Crampton kiosk at 11 a.m., Briggsby at noon and then back home to book off duty precisely at 1 p.m. 'Point' was the name we used to indicate the time and place we had to be for a possible rendezvous with the sergeant or other senior officer. During this patrol, I would visit a few outlying farms to check some stock registers and discuss the renewal of one or two firearms certificates.

At ten minutes to nine, I went into my little office which adjoined the police house at Aidensfield and telephoned the police station at Ashfordly. This was a daily ritual to see whether any messages awaited me. I was given a list of stolen vehicles, details of a couple of overnight crimes, and the description of a missing woman. It was a very routine start to my day.

I had to depart from my house at nine o'clock precisely. All my supervisory officers, and Sergeant Blaketon in particular, were keen on precise timing. Nine o'clock meant exactly that, not a minute past nine nor even a minute *to* nine. And I knew Sergeant Blaketon was on duty this morning; that meant he could be sitting outside my house in his official car, checking on whether or not I had managed to climb out of bed following my 1 a.m. finish this same morning. In his mind, punctuality was of paramount importance, and I do believe we sacrificed many fruitful enquiries and duties in order to be at a specific place at a specific time, just in case Oscar Blaketon was checking.

But on this fine spring morning things were going to plan. I had my cap on, my notebook was up to date and everything was in order by two minutes to nine. I kissed Mary and the children goodbye, still not comprehending the menace of Elizabeth's knowing grin. I went into the office for my van keys – I kept them on a hook under the counter.

They weren't there. They were not hanging in their usual place. I was sure I'd put them there last night when coming off duty. It was where I always hung them. I checked my uniform pockets without success, then rushed upstairs to see if they were on the bedside cabinet. They weren't. I checked my pockets again . . . then the bedroom floor, the bathroom floor . . . downstairs into the kitchen, into the downstairs loo, back to the office again . . .

'Have you seen the van keys?' I shouted to Mary as the clock struck nine. She was busy in the kitchen, washing the breakfast pots.

'You always put them on that hook in your office.'

'I know, but they're not there.'

'They must have fallen off. You're so careful with your keys, especially official ones,' came the voice from the kitchen.

'Then you haven't seen them?'

'No, I never do! I have no need to.'

'I haven't put them down on the draining-board or the breakfast table, have I?'

'No, I've cleared the table, I'd have seen them.'

I groaned. I decided to peep outside to see if Sergeant Blaketon had arrived. Fortunately, he had not. The coast was clear, which allowed me a few more minutes to continue my frantic search. I retraced my routine procedures, checking all the likely places again and again, and it was then that I realized that Elizabeth was following me around and scrutinizing all my actions – grinning the whole time.

'Elizabeth,' I asked, halting a moment in my anguish, 'have you seen daddy's keys? The keys for the police van?'

She clenched her lips and smiled in her silence. Mary had come through to my office at this stage and witnessed this behaviour. Elizabeth's grin was rather like that of the Mona Lisa with teeth.

'Elizabeth?' Mary recognized the mischief in that smile. 'Have you got daddy's keys?'

The response was a more firmly clenched mouth and fixed smile, with her tiny, round face going red with the effort of containing herself.

'Look, Elizabeth,' I said, 'Daddy's got to go to work and he must have the van keys. He can't get into the van without them – he can't switch the radio on and can't go to work.'

There was a spare set of keys, but they were kept on a board in the sergeants' office at Ashfordly police station, and I had no wish to allow Oscar Blaketon to learn of my dilemma by requesting them.

'Elizabeth,' Mary now took up the challenge, 'if you have got daddy's van keys, you must say so. He has to go to work, and the sergeant will be very cross if he doesn't go out in the van. Now, where are they?'

'April Fool, Daddy!' she grinned, her tight little mouth now opening as she could contain herself no longer. 'Daddy's an April Foo-hool!' she chanted.

I should have realized; I should have connected her wicked grins with the arrival of All Fool's Day, but I had not. I had to laugh at my own stupidity. I'd been well and truly caught.

'All right, Elizabeth, you made daddy an April Fool. Now, can I have the keys?'

'I have to keep them hidden till twelve o'clock,' she said solemnly. 'You're not a real April Fool if you get them back before twelve o'clock, and I know when twelve o'clock is. It's when both pointers are on twelve.'

'No, Elizabeth, you mustn't,' I tried to reason with her. 'You have made an April Fool out of daddy because he could not find the keys, so you've won. Now, I'd like my keys.'

'They said at school to wait till twelve o'clock,' she announced, that resolute line appearing on her face. 'And I'm not telling you where the keys are, Daddy.'

'Elizabeth . . .'

'You're an April Fool if you can't find them!' she began to chant.

Then the telephone rang.

'You answer it,' I entreated Mary. 'If it's the office, tell them I'm on patrol. Say I went out at nine.'

Mary did so. I heard her announcing that to whoever was calling, and she came back to say, 'It was Eltering office. You haven't booked on the air. They were checking.'

'They've booked me on now, have they?'

'They said it must be bad reception. Come on, Elizabeth, don't be silly . . .'

'I am not being silly!' she stamped her feet. 'April Fooling daddy is not silly. Everybody will be doing it.'

It became very evident that Elizabeth was not going to reveal her hiding-place. It was no good wasting time arguing – time was pressing and I had to do something positive. I did consider making all the clocks and watches show the time as twelve o'clock but I didn't think that would fool her. My only option was to go on patrol, otherwise I could be in serious trouble from Sergeant Blaketon and, because the van was now out of commission, I needed some alternative transport. I decided to use my own car, hiding it where necessary. I could make those hourly points, and if any senior officer challenged me, I could claim either that the radio reception was poor or that my van would not start. Both were correct! And then, after twelve noon, I could return home when, hopefully, Elizabeth would return my keys.

As Elizabeth stood with a grin of triumph upon her face, I knew I should remonstrate with her, and yet it seemed such a cruel thing to do when she was flushed with triumph. I could not be angry with her, not now. My own frustration had evaporated, and so I decided I would regard her triumph as a genuine victory. I praised her for her cleverness and headed for my car.

Fortunately, she had not hidden its keys, and so I made my way to the first point. I must admit I did so with some trepidation because, if the office had been trying to raise me on the radio, I would be subjected to a form of inquisition. But as I stood beside the telephone box at Elsinby there was no phone call and no visit from the ever-vigilant Sergeant Blaketon. From ten o'clock until eleven, I continued to visit outlying farms in my own car, the change in my transport not causing a flicker of interest in the farmers upon whom I called. At eleven, there was no telephone call at Crampton kiosk and I decided that, immediately after my noon point at Briggsby, I would drive home, hopefully to retrieve the keys from Elizabeth so that I could complete my tour of duty in official transport. Looking back upon the events of that morning, I suppose I had a charmed existence, because there were no official calls at the telephone kiosks, which in turn meant no one had been endeavouring to raise me on the radio.

Having completed my noon point, therefore, again with no calls from the office, I rushed home. Upon my return, Elizabeth was waiting with a triumphant smirk on her little face, and I admitted to her that I was an April Fool of the very best kind. I had not been able to prevent her trick from enduring until noon, and I knew I should be the subject of some discussion at school on Monday.

'So, Elizabeth,' I smiled, 'where are my van keys, please?'

'I was a very good hider, wasn't I?' she smiled at me.

'Yes, you were,' I had to agree. 'A very good hider indeed. Now, I must finish my tour of duty, Elizabeth, so can you get daddy's keys, please?'

'I've forgotten where I put them.' She stuck a finger in her mouth as she stared at me.

'But you can't . . . Mary!' I shouted. 'Mary, now she can't remember where she's hidden my keys!'

'Never mind, darling,' Mary patted me on the shoulder. 'You go and finish this patrol, and I'm sure Elizabeth and I can find your silly old keys.'

So I completed that patrol in my own car, and it was with some relief that I eased into my drive prompt at one o'clock to book off duty. I went into my office, happy that I'd been able to check a great many outstanding stock registers. Before lunch, I settled down to finalize my notebook with entries of my day's duties.

As I worked, Mary came in, albeit a little sheepishly.

'Darling,' she began, and I knew from the tone of her voice that there was a problem. 'Darling, I'm afraid Elizabeth genuinely can't remember where she's hidden your keys.'

As I groaned, the telephone rang. It was Sergeant Blaketon.

'Rhea?' he bellowed into the telephone. 'Where the devil have you been? We've been trying to raise you on the radio for the last twenty minutes. You are the only patrol on duty in the section. I need assistance.'

'Sorry, Sergeant,' I said. 'There was bad atmospherics . . . reception was poor all morning . . .'

'Yes, I guessed that. So get yourself down to Brantsford immediately. I need assistance, urgently.'

'Right, Sergeant,' I acknowledged. 'What is your location in Brantsford?'

'The police office, Rhea. Rendezvous there.'

I puzzled over his problem and had no alternative but to forgo my lunch and rush off in my own car. This morning's episode was costing me a fortune in petrol. Fifteen minutes later I parked on the hardstanding outside Brantsford police station and went in to meet the sergeant. He had heard my arrival, but his own problems were such that he apparently did not notice I was not in the official van.

'Sergeant?' I rushed into the office where he was waiting for me.

'Ah Rhea, sorry to drag you from your lunch, but I'm the victim of an April Fool's joke. Some idiot has let all my tyres down. I need help to change the wheels. The jack won't go under the car . . . and I need assistance to get them all blown up.'

Had I been in the mini-van, I knew that its jack would have been useless for this task, but I did have my own hydraulic jack. It was in the boot of my car. It was not issued with the vehicle but was my own property, a most useful present from my father. And so, my using that piece of equipment, I helped him raise the official car off the ground, first removing the two rear wheels, which we had inflated by a local garage, then the front ones and finally the spare, which was softer than it should have been. It was a long job.

'Thank you, Rhea,' he said when it was all over. 'I do hate being the subject of such pranks. Perhaps we can forget this ever happened, eh? As colleagues? As man to man?'

'I'm sure we can, Sergeant,' I agreed, wondering how long it would take me to recover my own official keys from Elizabeth's hiding-place. If that took a long time, I would need his co-operation. One good April Fool's joke deserved another, I felt.

But I needn't have worried. Mary found the keys after lunch. Elizabeth had hidden them in the ironing-board. There was a small hole in the cover, just large enough to slide in the keys from a mini van. Elizabeth, having remembered that Mary had once lost a brooch in there, had considered it a perfect hiding-place for the mini-van keys. Mary had found them as she'd lifted the ironing-board from its parking place – the keys had jingled in their secret nest.

I put them in my pocket and made a resolution not to leave them on the hook on All Fool's Day next year, and to cut myself a spare copy of them, just in case.

My short involvement with Sergeant Blaketon that day did have its merits. That night, he told me to finish an hour earlier than usual on my second tour, a 10 p.m. to 2 a.m. shift. He would cover the extra hour, he said, so my 1 a.m. finish was a thank-you from him.

It was highly appreciated as I curled up in bed against Mary's warm body for an extra hour on a cool spring morning. I thought Elizabeth had done me a good turn after all.

Practical jokes, were not, however, restricted to April Fool's Day. Although some were fun, others could be malicious. In reflecting upon Sergeant Blaketon's four flat tyres, I did wonder whether they were the result of a real joke or whether they were an act of malice. I had a sneaking suspicion they were the latter.

From time to time, reports of acts of a malicious but supposedly jocular nature were received at our offices. Quite often, they were perpetrated by one neighbour upon another usually from spite or revenge. We dealt with damaged cars, paint sprayed on doors or gates, damaged garden plants or greenhouses, broken windows and a host of petty nuisances. The perpetrators regarded them as jokes, the victims regarded them as menacing, and the police regarded them as a crime of malicious damage. Some perpetrators were never prosecuted because there was insufficient evidence to support a court appearance, even though the villain was known.

One such troublesome series of pranks occurred at Elsinby; it caused me a lot of work before I eventually traced and dealt with the culprit. During my enquiries, I was to learn that a lot of incidents had happened at the Hopbind Inn before I was made aware of them. For example, one trick was to lash the bumpers of parked cars to benches outside the pub. When a driver set off home at closing time, he would find himself towing a bench along the High street – which did not do much good to the bench. Then the pranks grew more serious. One car bumper was lashed to that of a car parked behind it, and so a tug-of-war developed between the two vehicles, sometimes resulting in the separation of the said bumper from the car.

It was at this stage that the landlord, George Ward, told me of these occurrences. He stressed that this was not an official complaint. Indeed, he was not the victim; his customers were the victims. He was merely making me aware of the on-going series of pranks because of their nuisance value.

Strictly speaking, it was no concern of mine unless and until I received a formal complaint from one of the 'injured persons', as we termed all victims of crime whether or not they suffered physically. After this unofficial notification, though, whenever I paid a visit to the Hopbind Inn, whether on duty or not, I would discreetly ask whether further pranks had been played. It seemed they came in short bursts and always under cover of darkness. Weeks would pass without anything happening, and then there would be a series of related incidents all within, say, a week. Then there would be another lull until a further outbreak occurred.

It seemed almost as if the joker was producing new ideas which he would use for a few days before turning to something else – when the lashed bumper-bar idea had run its course, he spent a week smearing windscreens with grease. After that, he switched on the cars' headlights so that the batteries became exhausted. Flat tyres were deployed, as were eggs broken upon roofs, or dustbin lids roped to the rear wheels – the clatter they made as the wheels turned was unbelievable.

From my point of view, there was one interesting feature: none of the pranks was truly malicious. For example, the tyres were not slashed, the cars' paintwork was not dented or scraped with coins, their petrol tanks were not filled with sugar, and their engines not interfered with. In other words, these were fairly harmless pranks which did not result in permanent damage. They were little more than a nuisance.

I patrolled the area whenever I was on duty, sometimes concealing myself in the churchyard or among shrubs and trees which allowed me to observe the pub and its car-park. Like the villain, I operated under cover of darkness, but I never saw any of these acts committed. Neither did anyone else – the prankster was never seen. This was odd. He seemed to know when he was able to operate. If only I could catch him in the act, I could threaten him with prosecution, and that would surely halt this silly behaviour.

Over the duration of these pranks, I never received any official complaint from the victims, and I regarded this as an acceptance of their minor nature. But they did become more serious as time went by. On one occasion, the door handle of a small van was lashed to the wooden framework of the porch of the inn – and when the van set off, down came the porch. Another time, one end of a rope was tied around one of the fence posts of the railings outside the inn, the other end being tied to a pick-up truck. And when the pick-up moved off, the railings were demolished. But even so, I never received any formal complaint, even though the regulars were aware of my interest. I did encourage them to make a report, but none did and I began to wonder why there persisted this apparent group reticence.

As the pranks continued, I received details through local gossip, and it was noteworthy that every incident occurred outside the Hopbind Inn. Nothing of this kind happened inside the pub, nor did the pranks extend into other areas of the village. From time to time, I discussed them with George, the landlord, and he accepted they were a nuisance but that no one seemed unduly bothered.

Then there was a fairly serious event. Outside the pub, on its extensive forecourt, were two petrol pumps. In addition to filling his customers with ale, George would also fill their cars with petrol, and the prankster chose to lash a tractor to one of those pumps. He had used a strong rope which he'd found on the tractor, and when the machine set off, it almost dragged the petrol pump to the ground and nearly fractured the pipes inside. This time, George decided to report it to me and to make it official.

'If you'd reported it earlier, George, I could have arranged long-term observations with my colleagues. We might have stopped these goings-on by now. There's a limit to the time I can spend sitting in bushes.'

'We don't want official action taking, Mr Rhea,' he said. 'We want it dealt with without any court appearances or owt like that.'

'But I can't taken an official report from you on those terms, George. Once I've made it formal, I will have to take the culprit to court, if we track him down.'

'Then I withdraw my official complaint, Mr Rhea. Look,

you are our local bobby, surely you can stop this carry-on before it gets out of hand, before real damage is done or somebody gets hurt?'

'I can't stop it, George, if I don't know who's involved. I must catch him in the act if I am to stop him. I've kept observations out there for weeks now, I've asked questions around the village, but no one tells me who's doing these things. We all know it's going on and has been going on for weeks, but no one will tell me who's behind it. I suspect you all know . . .'

He regarded me steadily. 'Aye,' he said. 'We all know but we don't want the lad taken to court.'

'Then if you know, you'll have had words with him yourselves?'

'Aye, lots of us have spoken to him, but it only makes him worse.'

'I think you and I had better have a long talk, George,' I said.

'Then you'd better come in, Mr Rhea.'

Over a coffee in his private lounge, George told me the story. His first statement confirmed something I had suspected for a while – that all the victims were related.

'They're all cousins, half-cousins and even quarter-cousins,' he said. 'Except me. Those whose cars were tied up or messed up are all related.'

'A local family?' I asked.

'Aye, all living hereabouts. They're all Pattons, but some have different names through marrying.'

'So is the culprit a Patton or from another family who's got some grudge against them?' I asked.

'He's one of the Pattons,' he said, clearly expecting me to know which one. But there was a huge family whose members were spread right across the dale and the moors beyond. I knew several of them, albeit not very well, but could not guess which was the phantom prankster.

'I'm sorry, George. I don't know all the Pattons, and I have no idea which is the troublemaker.'

'It's young Noel,' he said. 'We all know it's him; mind, nobody's caught him at it, nor even seen him.'

'So how do they know?' I asked.

'It's common knowledge in the family.' George poured me a second coffee. 'The lad's not all there, if you know what I mean. He's not daft enough to be certified or sent into a mental institution, but he was at the back of the queue when God was dishing brains out. He's about eleven pence to the shilling. He works on one of the family farms, Dykegate Farm, labouring, doing basic jobs, and he bikes there every day.'

'That's off my patch.' I knew the farm, but it was on the beat of a neighbouring constable. 'So where's he live?'

'Pattington, in Long Row, number eight. With his mum. She's a Patton – not married, by the way.'

'So he's got no dad?'

'It's worse than that, Mr Rhea. They reckon Noel's dad was her own brother.'

'So he's the product of incest!'

I could now understand why the family did not want this lad prosecuted. If he appeared before a court, his family history would have to be presented to the magistrates, and no one wanted to open up old secrets or have the family's shame discussed in the pages of the local press. As Pattington was off my patch and in a different police division, I had never visited the village on duty, and this explained why I did not know the lad or his family.

'Aye, it was a sad thing, but the father is now married and working not far away. He's one of the Pattons, well respected, a chapel-goer an' all,' said George. 'His wife doesn't know Noel's his son; outsiders all think he's a nephew.'

'Well, he is!' I put to George. 'He's the fellow's nephew as well as his son!'

'You wouldn't think he was any relation, the way some of the Pattons treat him. They treat him like a dog at times, they tolerate him around, no one really loves him. Even his mother tries to ignore him.'

This chat enabled me to understand the motive behind Noel's actions. He seemed to be getting at his family for their attitude towards him, and I could also understand the desire for family unity and secrecy. In spite of all this, I knew, for the sake of all, that Noel's silly behaviour must be halted. If he was allowed to continue his pranks, they would grow more daring and more serious until one day there would be a serious accident or injury.

'Does he come into your pub?' I asked George, for I wanted to have a look at this youth, so that I'd know him in the future.

He shook his head. 'His mother's a strict chapel woman,' he told me. 'Alcohol and pubs are not regarded as proper, so she's brought Noel up to believe drink is evil – mebbe she was drunk when he was conceived . . . or his dad might have been. His real dad won't go into a pub but drinks whisky at home, gallons of it. He buys it from me, telephones his order in and the shop delivers it with the groceries. He thinks it's all a secret. Anyroad, Noel never comes in either. I think that might be a motive for his tricks as well. Mebbe he's getting at those of his clan who do indulge in evil spirits!'

I thanked George for his wealth of knowledge and told him I appreciated his confiding in me. Now that I was aware of the background, it explained a lot and was helpful – but how could I halt Noel's silly behaviour?

In the weeks that followed, he played more tricks: balloons appeared on one car, another's windows were painted with white emulsion, and a chunk of wallpaper was glued to the door of yet another. I attributed all this to Noel, even though I had never set eyes on the lad, for all the cars belonged to members of the Patton family.

I kept observation on the pub forecourt without ever catching sight of Noel, and I did have words with the village constable for Pattington and explained the situation to him. He knew Noel but said the lad never caused any trouble on his patch. I learned he was in his early twenties, fairly tall and slim, with long blond hair, and he rode a red bike with dropped handlebars.

Then, quite by chance, I was off duty in Ashfordly and doing some shopping in Thompson's hardware shop when I became aware of the presence of a young man of that description. He was selecting various objects from the shelves and popping them into a basket – they were things like shelf-brackets, wall plugs, screws and other DIY items. I peeped outside the large window and saw a red racing bike propped against the wall. So this was young Patton, I guessed. Then he went to the counter and asked for a box of 200 rounds of .22 ammunition.

'Have you your certificate?' the shopkeeper asked.

It is illegal to sell such ammunition to anyone who is not the holder of a firearms certificate, and the seller must endorse the certificate with the amount and type he sells. This does not apply to shotgun ammunition, nor pellets for air weapons, but it does strictly apply for ammunition – i.e. bullets – for use with rifles and such handguns as revolvers and pistols. Clearly, this lad had such a weapon.

I hovered behind a tall display stand and listened. This knowledge would be of use to me.

'I haven't a certificate,' said the youth. 'I allus uses my uncle's bullets. He lets me.'

'Who's rifle is it?' asked the shopkeeper.

'Mine,' said Noel. 'Me grandad gave me it.'

'Well, you must have a certificate for the rifle, so fetch that in and I can let you have the bullets.'

'No,' said the lad. 'I've no certificate for t'gun, never 'ave had. I just have it and borrow bullets. But I thought I'd try to buy some for myself. I am over seventeen, so how can I get this certificate?'

'You'll have to apply to the police,' said the shopkeeper. 'And if they think you are a fit and proper person to possess such a firearm, you will be granted a certificate.'

'Aye, right,' said Noel, paying for his odds and ends.

When he left the shop, I followed. I could not let this opportunity pass without making use of it.

As he placed his purchases in the pannier behind the saddle, I said, 'Hello, are you Noel Patton?'

'Aye.' He stood up and looked at me, a puzzled expression on his face. I was not wearing uniform.

'I'm PC Rhea from Aidensfield,' I introduced myself. 'Part of my responsibility is the Hopbind Inn at Elsinby.'

'Oh aye.' He looked me up and down but gave nothing away.

'I have reason to believe you have been making a nuisance of yourself there, playing tricks on cars and things.'

He said nothing. Simple though he might be, he was shrewd and cunning, I realized.

'All I want to say, Noel, is that it must stop. No more pranks, no more jokes on your family or their cars when they're at the pub. No more ropes tied to bumpers, petrol pumps and the like.'

'Who said it were me?' he suddenly shouted.

'It doesn't matter who said it was. I know it was. All I'm saying is that it must stop. Right now, as from today. No more pranks, right?'

'Nobody's seen me, nobody knows . . .'

'I know it's you, Noel, and so do lots of other folks. Now, I happen to know you have a rifle without a certificate. I could get you sent to prison for that.'

'Grandad gave it to me. It's from the big war.'

'No matter, you must have a certificate. Now, as I said, I'm the policeman at Aidensfield, and if there are any more pranks outside the Hopbind, I'll take you to court for having that gun without a certificate. Do you understand?'

'Prison?' he gasped.

'If you misbehave,' I said grimly. I had over-emphasized the penalties but felt it justified if it stopped his antics.

'No more pranks then, Mr Policeman. I'm sorry. It's just they keep getting at me.'

'I'm sorry, but you mustn't take it out on them like that, Noel.'

'OK, I won't,' and he sat astride his bike, ready to ride off. 'So what about the gun then?'

I did wonder whether I should arrange for it to be confiscated but said, 'You apply for a certificate, and your local bobby will send it to our headquarters. Then you'll be able to keep that gun.' I knew that by this procedure he would be carefully vetted by his local policeman.

'Right,' and off he rode.

A couple of months passed without incident and then, when I was standing outside the telephone kiosk at Elsinby, awaiting any call that might come, Noel rode up on his red bike. He halted at my side.

'Mr Rhea,' he said, surprising me because he remembered my name, 'that gun o' mine. Me mum wouldn't let me apply for a certificate, nor would my Uncle Jack. They said I had no need, I could use the farm guns for killing rabbits and pigeons . . .'

'So you'll have handed in your rifle, have you? To your local policeman?'

'No, I've buried it.'

'Buried it? Where?'

'There's a deep bog in Ferrers Wood. I pushed it right down, used a rake handle to make sure it went real deep, then all t'watter covered it up. Nobody'll find it there, Mr Rhea, nobody.'

I knew he was telling the truth.

'Thanks for telling me, Noel. Maybe that was the wisest thing to do.'

'Mum said it was.' He smiled and rode off towards Pattington.

And there was no more pranks on the Patton cars when they parked outside the Hopbind Inn at Elsinby.

5 *The Storeman Syndrome*

I question if keeping it does much good.
Revd Richard Harris Barham (1788–1845)

In the middle years of this century, there existed within the police service – and probably within many other organizations – a philosophy that, if you wanted something which would improve your conditions or make your work easier or more efficient, you should not be allowed to have it.

I am sure that notion still persists, although there has been an improvement in many aspects of the police administration. Once it was believed that those who funded the police service would love and cherish officers who could spend the least. Now the idea is that you spend as much as possible in order to convince the authorities that more money is always needed if efficiency is to be maintained or improved.

I think the logic behind the earlier financially repressive thinking was simply that it saved money. Certainly lots of people asked lots of questions if official money was freely spent; few seemed to realize that a police force has all the financial needs and expenditure of any other large organization. A lot of the blame must rest upon those senior officers who, unlike Oliver Twist, were afraid to ask for more. They were allocated a budget and constantly struggled to function within its limitations. What they should have done is spent more to prove that the funds were inadequate for their needs. But they would never ask for more, because they thought it was an admission of failure, which meant that those of us lower down the scale had to make do and improvise.

One glaring example presented to us immediately upon joining the force was that we were issued with second-hand uniforms. I think the force tailor thought that all police officers were six foot six inches high, sixteen-stone giants with chests like barrels. Certainly all the second-hand uniforms seemed tailored for men of that ilk, and all recruits were issued with them. It was thought they would never dare complain.

If, for example, your uniform jacket was large enough to accommodate a pregnant hippopotamus, you had to tolerate its shapelessness and size because the effort of exchanging it for one more comfortable involved much expense and paperwork. To point out its defects labelled you a rebel; it also suggested that the man in charge of issuing uniforms (usually a sergeant) had been inefficient in giving you something that did not fit, and such overt criticism could ruin one's prospects. Original thinkers were considered subversives who had no part in the police service, and such outrageous requests or ideas were not tolerated. The result was that we never complained about our appearance because we dare not.

As a consequence, many police officers plodded around the streets in badly fitting, second-hand uniforms that gave the wearer's rear end the appearance of a sauntering elephant with an overweight problem. Those who wonder why uniformed policemen suddenly bend their knees and flex their legs to give the appearance of a diamond-shaped ballet pose, while quothing 'Hello, Hello', may now appreciate that it has something to do with ill-fitting trousers.

Proud wives, mothers or girlfriends with needlework skills did sometimes try to improve this baggy frippery, but some policemen did not benefit from such caring love. They walked around like pantalooned scarecrows in the belief that the secret of smartness was to cut your hair, clean your boots and press your trousers from time to time; any other aspects of dress were not important. There was, however, an implication that, if your uniform fitted perfectly, you were deformed.

Having been nurtured to this philosophy, it was with some surprise that I once entered the camphor-scented uniform store at force headquarters to find it stocked to the ceiling with brand-new uniforms in a range of interesting and even useful sizes. But I was to learn that these were never issued – they were stored, and I then discovered that that is precisely the function of stores and storemen. Their mission in life is to store things, not to issue them, and the Storeman Syndrome exists at all levels of the service, and in all departments. This is true in many other large organizations storemen and storewomen make it very difficult to draw items from their cherished stock. They produce a mass of schemes and procedures which are designed to prevent the staff's having the necessities of their calling.

I recall one police officer who was in charge of stores when ballpoint pens became fashionable. It was deemed by someone in authority that all officers should be issued with an official ballpoint pen. Progress had at last arrived within the service, because ballpoints would write in the rain without smudging the page – and that was a massive step forward for the busy outdoor constable. Making a neat and legible fountain pen entry in one's notebook on a rainy day was, until then, almost impossible, and so ballpoints revolutionized police work. But this giant stride towards the twentieth century had not reckoned with the Storeman Syndrome. Our storemen did not believe that ballpoints could run dry without warning when out in the town – it seemed they were always supposed to run dry when you were in the office, because you were not allowed a refill until the old one actually ceased to function. How one was supposed to take statements and make notes when on town duty with a pen devoid of ink was never decided, but the storeman said you could have a replacement refill only when the first one became exhausted – and application for that refill had to be made in writing.

'But, Sergeant,' I said when I was a mere 16-year-old cadet, 'how can I apply in writing if the pen's run dry?'

'We'll have none of that clever stuff here, young Rhea,' he said.

I went out and bought my own supply of ballpoints – which, on reflection, is precisely what the Storeman Syndrome seeks to achieve. If everyone behaved like that, many pens would be stored and never issued. In the older police stations of this kingdom, there must be mountains of unused ballpoint pens of a most ancient style, memorials to past and diligent storemen.

Upon being transferred to Aidensfield, I thought I would experience an end of the Storeman Syndrome, for our local section station was Ashfordly. Surely the sergeants in such a small and friendly station would look after their men and be willing to issue them with all their routine necessities?

But I hadn't bargained for Sergeant Blaketon.

When I first arrived, I did not require any stores, because my predecessor had stocked my office shelves – a kind touch, I felt. I had a plentiful supply of official forms, envelopes, a rubber, a few ballpoints, chalk (for marking the road at the scene of a traffic accident), a ruler and other office and operational essentials. Looking back, I have no idea how the previous Aidensfield constable had managed to stockpile such quantities – he must have raided the store while Sergeant Blaketon was on holiday.

I was soon to learn that Sergeant Blaketon took his storeman duties most seriously. He alone kept the key to the stores; it could be used by others only after signing for it in 'the Store Key Book', and such signings had to be witnessed in writing by another officer. It had then to be recorded in that book precisely what had been removed from the store, each person present witnessing the honesty of the transaction. Inside the store, there was another book. This one listed every single object in the stores, and the entries created a series of running totals. On one occasion, I saw he had four gross tins of Vim and 250 floor-cloths – I reckoned these would keep our cells scoured well into the twenty-first century. These ponderous procedures were to counteract any suggestion of pilfering by the local constables.

On one occasion I was privileged to sneak a rare peep into Sergeant Blaketon's store. That was when I realized it was there – what I had originally thought to be a small cupboard in the wall of his office was in reality a spacious storeroom. When the door was opened, it led into a type of cupboard-under-the-stairs. It ran the length of the sergeant's office wall and was about six feet wide, extending under his private accommodation at Ashfordly police station. It was a veritable Aladdin's Cave, stocked with everything from mop handles to pencil-sharpeners, by way of ink wells, toilet rolls and tins of furniture polish. A quick appraisal of the contents showed that some stock had been there since the foundation of the North Riding Constabulary in 1856 and were now museum pieces. Examples included acetylene cycle lamps, pen-holders and nibs, two spare whistle chains, a tin of black lead and other assorted gems.

The only reason I managed to see these cherished stocks was that, at the precise moment Sergeant Blaketon opened the door, his telephone rang. Thus I had a few brief moments of ecstasy as with a worried frown on his face, he watched my antics. My only purpose in being there was to obtain a new notebook, which I did after signing for it. I'm sure he thought I was scheming to pilfer something.

I recall two supreme examples of Sergeant Blaketon's own individual flair in storemanship. The first involved an electric light bulb.

Those of us with office accommodation adjoining our private houses were instructed to obtain official bulbs for the office. I think this was to prevent some of us making an application for an office bulb allowance. I would have been quite happy to furnish a bulb from my own funds, but orders are orders. Consequently, when my office bulb began to flicker, I thought it was time for a new one. When I was next in Ashfordly police station, I made my request.

'I need a new bulb for the office, Sergeant,' I began.

'Size?' asked Sergeant Blaketon.

'100 watt.'

'We don't stock hundreds. You'll have to make do with a 60 watt,' he said.

'That's not very bright if I'm working at night,' I said.

'Economy, Rhea, economy. We can't go around dishing out big bulbs when smaller wattages will do. Now, you've brought your old one in?'

'No, Sergeant. It's not finished yet, it's flickering. I think it might go out soon. I want to be prepared.'

'But if your present one is still working, why do you want a replacement?'

I groaned inwardly. Here was the Storeman Syndrome in all its perfection.

'It's nearly done, Sergeant. It's been used ever since I came to Aidensfield, and it's flickering, like they do just before they pack up. I thought I'd be prepared for when it does fizzle out.

I don't want to be caught out at night with no bulb if you're not around to issue one.'

'You know I can't issue a new bulb without taking in the old one,' he said. 'That is my system. New for old.'

I knew his system. He thought that if he issued something new without inspecting the expired old equivalent, the new thing would be purloined for the private use of the officer, who would later return for another new one. And so production of the old was an indication of total honesty. Men like Oscar Blaketon don't even trust themselves.

'So what happens if it goes out when I'm in the middle of an urgent report?'

'You've got bulbs at home, haven't you? In the house? Borrow one of those until you get the official one replaced.'

'That'll mean my family might have to cope with the dark!'

'But that is not my problem, Rhea,' he smirked. 'I have no interest in your domestic problems. So that's it – when your bulb blows, come to me for a new one, and fetch the old one in, as proof.'

And having said that, he refused to change his tactics.

The next example involved No. 1 cell. There were two cells at Ashfordly police station, No. 1 being the male cell and No. 2 the female cell. They were rarely, if ever, used by prisoners, because we seldom arrested anyone at Ashfordly, but we did make use of the toilet in No. 1, because the cell toilets were the only ones in the police station. While on duty one day, I had occasion to visit the loo in No. 1 and noticed that the toilet roll was almost exhausted.

'Sergeant,' I later announced to Sergeant Blaketon, 'we need a new toilet roll in No. 1 cell.'

'Is it finished?' he asked.

'No, there's about three sheets left.'

'Then I'll issue one when it's exhausted. When it runs out, fetch me the cardboard tube from the roll.'

'But if you get a prisoner in who needs more than three sheets, he's going to be in a bit of a pickle, Sergeant,' I said. 'Or it could be one of us, alone in the station. If we put one out now, in reserve, like they do in hotels . . .'

'This is not an hotel, Rhea. This is a police station, and I issue new toilet rolls only on production of the used tube. Otherwise everybody would be asking for them.'

'Do you think we'd take them home or something, Sergeant?' In my exasperation I was cheeky to him.

'It has been known, Rhea,' was his cold reply. 'Just ask British Rail or any of your hotels . . .'

'I can't imagine any of our men wanting to make private use of this paper,' I laughed. 'It's nearly as bad as cutting up squares of the *Daily Mirror*.'

'I care not for your opinions or sarcasm, Rhea. My job is to maintain stocks of equipment and to issue it when needed. It is not my intention to squander official supplies. A new toilet roll is not needed yet.'

And that was that.

Ten minutes later I returned to the loo, used the three sheets and beamed at him as I held out the cardboard tube.

'I do trust you have not wasted official toilet paper, Rhea, in order to make your point,' he said as he handed me a new roll and booked it out.

'No, I've thrown it down the toilet, Sergeant,' I assured him. 'But before I left the cell, it did serve a useful purpose.'

For me, and indeed all the other constables in Ashfordly section, it became something of an ongoing challenge to persuade Sergeant Blaketon to part with any official stores. We used all sorts of devices and excuses in our attempts to win our deserved odds and ends, but his system reigned unconquered.

And then, to our delight, one market day, his stores were superbly raided.

I was on duty and was patrolling among the colourful stalls, savouring the atmosphere that is generated by this weekly conglomeration of fish, fruit and fancy goods, when a uniformed police constable hailed me.

I recognized him as the deputy chief constable's official driver but did not know his name.

'Ah,' he said. 'Caught you. I'm PC Hughes, David Hughes. DCC's driver.'

'PC Rhea, Nicholas; Nick.' We shook hands.

'The boss spotted you as we drove past,' said Hughes. 'He asked me to take you back to the car.'

'Something wrong?' I wondered why on earth the deputy chief constable would want to talk to me. He wasn't in the habit of calling on constables like this.

'No. He wants to visit your office. There's no one in just now.'

I approached the gleaming black Humber Snipe, flung up a smart salute and said, 'Good morning, sir,' as he lowered his window.

'Hop in, Constable,' he invited, and so I did. As we cruised away, he said, 'I'm in the area and thought I'd give the station an official visit. It's locked.'

'Sergeant Bairstow is on day off, sir,' I told him. 'And Sergeant Blaketon went over to Brantsford.'

'And you are PC Rhea, eh?'

'Yes, sir,' I replied, wondering how he knew my name. I was later to learn he had an amazing memory for numbers – he'd seen the numerals on my shoulders. He was a charming man, easy-going but efficient.

When we arrived at the station, I unlocked the door and escorted him inside. PC Hughes waited outside in the official car. The DCC examined the cells, the books, the general state of the place and the daily occurrence book. In keeping with the procedures for such a visit, he would then make an entry in the occurrence book to record the event.

'Well, your sergeants and colleagues keep the place in good order, PC Rhea,' he said. 'I wish all our stations were so efficiently kept. Now, I'll just sign your occurrence book and then I'll be on my way.' And he began to tap his pockets as he sought a pen. 'Damn,' he said. 'I must have left my pen in the office.'

'You can borrow mine, sir,' and I produced my ballpoint.

'I'll need one for the rest of the day,' he said. 'Can you issue me with one from your stock?'

I explained Sergeant Blaketon's book procedures, and the DCC smiled. 'I'll witness your signature for the issue of one ballpoint to me,' he said, with just a trace of humour in his eyes. But when I opened the cupboard door and stepped inside, he followed and exclaimed, 'Well, I'll be damned! This is like a museum!'

He went inside and picked things off the shelves to examine them, chuckling and shaking his head as he found treasures from a bygone age. There was even an old-fashioned stalk telephone, a copper kettle, a leather-bound book with no entries at all, a Victorian pen-holder and stacks of old files.

'PC Rhea,' he said suddenly, 'am I right in thinking there was a charity stall on your market-place today as I came past?'

'Yes, sir. It's for the parish church. They're raising funds to repair the bell tower.'

'Then all this surplus stuff must go. Have it taken to the stall now and get rid of it. It is no use here; in fact, I issued an instruction several months ago for all such clutter to be cleared out. This lot will help a deserving cause.'

'I'll inform Sergeant Blaketon, sir.'

'It's no good relying on old Oscar, PC Rhea. I served with him at Scarborough years ago. I know him too well. No, we'll do it now, you, me and PC Hughes.'

And so we did. We loaded the rear seat and the boot of the DCC's official car with what amounted to a cache of antiques and surplus but unused domestic goods of ages past, such as old tins of polish and brush-heads. The stallholder was delighted. The DCC left a note for Sergeant Blaketon to explain what he'd done, and I resumed my patrol.

Later Sergeant Blaketon said nothing to me, and when I did next peer into his cupboard, I saw he'd used the space to accommodate more stocks. Among the boxes, I noticed three gross of toilet rolls. The one in No. 1 cell had just five sheets left, but even with such a colossal supply, I wasn't going to ask him for a replacement just yet.

When patrolling the moors around Aidensfield, I soon discovered that the Storeman Syndrome is not confined to those employed in formal organizations. It exists among individuals too. There are many examples of those who simply cannot throw anything away, in case it might come in useful for some obscure future purpose.

I have heard it said that everything comes in useful once every seven years. On one of my moves to another house, I found a coiled and lengthy piece of wire in an outbuilding. In its prime, it had been an old-fashioned television aerial. Following the belief that it might be useful one day, I kept it – and some ten years later found it ideal for cleaning out drains. Policemen do tend to keep things 'just in case'. Storerooms and cupboards throughout the land are full of things which are kept 'just in case'. It is true, of course, that, if one disposes of any one of these items, it will be required two or three days after the dustman has carted it away. That might explain why my garage is full of odd bits of apparently useless paraphernalia, all of which I believe have some potential destiny.

But scattered about the moors and dales are people who keep things for best, who reserve rooms for special events which seldom seem to happen, who keep drawers full of linen which is never used, and crockery which has never been sullied with food or drink. The front doors of such homes are rarely opened, and visitors are invariably welcomed in the kitchen. Even now, I find myself in this category – our callers come to the kitchen door. It's a matter of custom, not discrimination. In my tours of duty I had occasion to visit many such places and came to realize that it was not an unusual aspect of moorland life. In fact, it was very much a part of the prevailing practice.

The typical situation was like this. A householder or family living on a farm, or in a country house or cottage, would live in the kitchen. This was a plain, functional place, often with a bare stone floor, but with a couple of Windsor chairs for comfort and with a bare wooden table for all meals. There was rarely a dining-room – all meals were taken in the kitchen. Elsewhere in the house would be a sitting-room; this was more comfortable, perhaps with rugs or even a carpet on the floor, settees and easy chairs and a welcoming fire. There would be sideboards too and pictures on the wall.

But in addition to these there was the best room, sometimes known as 'the house' or in some areas as 'the parlour'. This was often at the front of the house, close to the seldom-used front door. Judging from those I have seen, they were dark and airless and always smelt of mothballs. The window was never opened, the rooms usually faced north and so attracted little sunshine or light, and they were full of 'best' things which were to be used only on special occasions and which had, in many cases, been passed down from one generation to the next. Wonderful old antique furnishings, a firescreen, cushions, rugs, the carpet, easy chairs, crockery, drawers full of unopened linen such as pillowcases, sheets and serviettes, smart cutlery, a selection of ancient books, some antique ornaments, a piano, the family Bible and the inevitable, well-thumbed album of family photographs. Most rooms of this type that I had occasion to visit reeked of Victoriana and must have been an antique-collector's dream – in some there was even an aspidistra in a heavy brown pot. Throughout the life of the contents, they had seldom been used, having always been kept for best.

'Best' seemed to imply family gatherings such as christenings, weddings and funerals (especially funerals), although if an important visitor called, the room might be put into use. It would have to be someone very important indeed to justify preparation of that room, for the status of the visitor had to be substantial before the fire was lit and the room made welcoming. Routine calls by vicars, vets, van-drivers, valuers and visiting relations did not quality – there had to be something special about the call and the caller.

The degree of high importance was generally something associated with the family. I doubt whether the Queen, if she called without warning, would be shown into that room, and the same might be said of the lord of the manor, although if cousin Freda came all the way from Canada to trace the family tree, the lady of the house might get her duster out and 'do' that room.

If the room was maintained for very important family occasions, its contents were likewise separated from the rigours of the daily routine. Gifts given to the husband and wife at their wedding, for birthdays, at Christmas and anniversaries were seldom used – they were put away for a special occasion. Drawers in such rooms and indeed in bedrooms and other parts of the house contained unopened parcels dating from the wedding day of the occupiers. I found this an intriguing practice. Things needed from day to day, such as household crockery, were used with alacrity, but special things, such as presents, were never used – they were always put away. I was never quite sure why, although it happened with such regularity.

Having once been put away for a special occasion, such an item rarely saw service, because there was never an occasion special enough to justify unwrapping it or opening it. Whatever occurred never quite seemed to qualify for the ceremonial use of Aunt Emily's gift of china, Uncle Jasper's white sheets or Cousin Ermintrude's canteen of cutlery.

In contemplating this logic, I doubt if that predetermined visit by Her Majesty would be of sufficient importance to bring out such treasures. She'd probably be given a drink of tea in a mug bearing a picture of her grandmother, but she might be allowed to sit on the best sofa in the best room to sip it; if she came to a family funeral, however, the best room would be available.

Probably the most upsetting incident which involved such a room happened one hot July day. It was just after 10 a.m. and I was prepared to patrol Aidensfield and district in my little van when Dr Archie McGee from Elsinby knocked at the door. He was dressed in his plus-fours as usual, and I never knew whether he was doing his rounds or going shooting.

'Ah, Nick,' he beamed in his affable way. 'I've just driven past Mrs Gregory's place and there's a light on. I thought I'd mention it – she's away, you know. She's gone to her sister's funeral in Bradford.'

'It must be something serious to get her away from home,' I smiled. 'But how long's she been away?'

'Day before yesterday,' he said. 'I came past last night and there was no light.'

'Me too,' I said. 'I came past at half-past eleven last night, and it was all in darkness. Thanks, Doctor, I'll have a look. Did you stop at the house?'

'No,' he said. 'I've an appointment at Malton Hospital. Got to be going,' and off he went.

Mrs Gregory's house, known as Southview, was only a few hundred yards from my own police house, but I took the van because of its radio capability. I parked outside. It was a magnificent house, a stone-built double-fronted building with a tiled roof and oak windowframes. It stood in its own grounds and was tucked deep into the hillside midway down Aidensfield Bank, with expansive views to the south.

I knew Mrs Gregory by sight. She was a lady in her mid seventies, I guessed, and she had been a widow for years. She had no children, but I did know she had sisters in various parts of Yorkshire. The house revealed something of her status – although she was a Yorkshirewoman from a simple background, she had married well, because her house was what is often described as 'a gentleman's residence' or even 'a gentry house'. I knew little of her husband, for he had died long before my arrival in the village.

Upon leaving my van, I could see the light burning in one of the front rooms, so I knocked on the front door, and when there was no reply, I tried the back. Again there was no response, so I examined the windows. Those at the front and rear were secure but as I went around the side, where the house wall was literally a yard from the limestone cliff face near where it had been built, my heart sank. A small pantry window had been smashed and was standing open. I knew better than to climb in that way, for evidence of forensic interest might be adhering to the framework.

I returned to the doors and tried the knobs. The back door opened easily – the key was in the lock on the inside, and chummy had used this route as his exit. As I entered, aware of the need to proceed with great care, I knew the house had been burgled. My heart sank. This was probably the first time for years that Mrs Gregory had been away, and I could only feel deep sorrow on her behalf. But it was time to set in motion the official procedures and then to trace Mrs Gregory.

I did make a quick tour of the stricken house, just to ensure that the villain was not still hiding, and then closed the doors as I set in motion the investigation. I called the CID in Eltering, who said Detective Sergeant Gerry Connolly and Detective PC Paul Wharton would attend within the half hour. In the meantime, I left the van outside the house and walked down to the post office-cum-shop to ask Joe Steel if he knew how I could contact Mrs Gregory. He did; he gave me her sister's home number. I returned to the van and radioed Force Control, asking them to contact Mrs Gregory with the sad news and ask her to ring me before coming home. Then I stood outside the house to await the might of the local CID.

Connolly and Wharton came and commenced their investigation. The curious thing was the state of one room. The entire floor was covered with masses of wrapping paper and screwed-up newspaper. It covered the tops of flat surfaces, such as the table and sideboard, and even filled the spaces beneath chairs and bookcases. The room looked like an expanded version of our children's bedrooms on Christmas morning.

'What's all this, Nick?' asked Detective Sergeant Connolly, showing me the rubbish.

'No idea,' I had to admit. 'I've not been in the house until today.'

'It's neat and tidy otherwise, but we can't tell what's gone until she returns. Certainly the place has been done over, and it looks like an expert job. We've not found any marks.'

By that, he meant there were no fingerprints, which suggested the work of a professional thief rather than a local lad who had broken in for kicks.

'We'll be off, Nick,' said Connolly. 'Lock the house and then call us when she gets back – we'll find out what's gone then.'

When I got home, Mary said there'd already been a call from Mrs Gregory, and she would be home that evening around seven o'clock; in view of the awful news, her nephew was driving her home and would stay a day or two. I made sure I was at the house to meet them.

Mrs Gregory arrived in her nephew's Hillman Husky and headed straight for the front door. She was a sturdy woman of moorland stock, with iron-grey hair peeping from beneath a tight-fitting purple hat. She walked like a farm labourer, her stout legs carrying her quickly across the ground. She almost waddled into the house after nodding briefly to me. I followed her in, leaving her nephew to see to her luggage and the car.

'I'm sorry this has happened, Mrs Gregory.' I tried to reassure her but she seemed not to care. 'The CID have been. They've done their work but will have to visit you when you can tell them what's been taken.'

She buzzed from room to room, saying, 'Nowt from here, nowt from this 'un . . .' until she arrived at the room with all the waste paper on the floor.

'This is how we found it, Mrs Gregory. We've not touched anything.'

'They've had a right do in 'ere, eh?' she said. 'They've opened stuff I've had parcelled up since I was wed.'

She picked up one piece of ancient silver-coloured wrapping paper. 'Egg cups, I think,' she said. 'From this lot.'

I stood back as she examined the mess, and when her nephew came in, I suggested he make a cup of tea for us all. I learned his name was Robert Atkinson. Gradually she moved every piece of paper, and when she had finished, she led me into the kitchen, where Robert had prepared a cup of tea and some biscuits. It was an old-fashioned kitchen with a black-leaded fireside and beams overhead.

'It's all my wedding presents,' she said eventually. 'That's what he's got. Crockery, silverware, pots and pans, linen, glassware . . .'

'You mean you never used any of it, Mrs Gregory?'

'Never had the need,' she said. 'Allus had enough stuff without opening presents. Besides, my Alexander died two days after our wedding, so I never had the heart to open anything.'

'Oh, dear, I am sorry.'

'It was a long time ago,' she said. 'Long before you saw t'light of day, young man. He went off t'war, First World War that was, and got himself killed. Married for two days, I was. And so I never opened any of them presents. He left me well provided for.'

'What did he do? For a living?' I asked her as Robert poured the tea.

'He was in business, ironmongery. His family have a chain of shops in t'West Riding; they're still there. I get a pension from 'em, and I've shares. I'm all right for cash, Mr Rhea, and that stuff is all insured.'

'If I might say so, Mrs Gregory, you are taking this remarkable well.'

'It's no good doing any other,' she said. 'You can't make things better by worrying. I've never used any of that stuff, so

I shan't miss it. In fact, Mr Rhea, it's mebbe solved a problem. All them nephews and nieces o' mine might have fought over those things. Well, they can't now.'

'I'll need a list,' I said. 'To circulate through our channels, to other police forces and antique-dealers.'

'I'll have my wedding "thank-you" list somewhere,' she said. 'I can get a full list in a while.'

'We'll need a description of the objects,' I said. 'You know, any distinguishing marks, unusual designs, that sort of thing.'

I rang Gerry Connolly from her house and explained it would take a while for her to compile the list, but he was happy that she was able to do so at all; many in this situation might not know exactly what had been taken. I kept her company for about an hour and was delighted that she had been such a tower of strength in her loss.

As I got up to leave, she stooped and picked up a black-lead brush from the hearth.

'See this brush, Mr Rhea?'

'My granny had one like that,' I said.

'That was a wedding present,' she smiled. 'I use it every day. I'm right glad he never took that. You can't get good black-lead brushes like that nowadays.'

I left, marvelling that she had never had any use or joy from her wedding presents, save the black-lead brush.

As a postscript, we did recover several of her silver items, because they had been monogrammed by her late husband's family. They began to turn up in second-hand salerooms and antique shops in various parts of the country, but the thief was never arrested.

I think that, if he had stolen her black-lead brush, she would have been very upset. But we might not have recovered that – it didn't bear the family monogram.

6 *Kittens Among the Phobias*

Our antagonist is our helper.
Edmund Burke (1729–97)

There is no doubt that some people are truly afraid of police officers, and there are also some who dislike or even hate them. The reasons are many and varied.

From my own experiences, I found that political propaganda of the more sinister type is responsible for a large amount of fear and distrust, this often being based on one solitary act by a less-than-perfect officer or through well-chosen photographs of highly publicized confrontations. There is certainly a wealth of anti-police myth in some political circles through which gullible idealists grow to believe those who preach poison rather than those who are better equipped to reveal the truth. The trouble is that it is easy to accept the ravings of those who profess to know more than oneself. Enlightenment can come later, sometimes much later and sometimes too late, and it is often achieved when the disaffected one has been subjected to some experience which starkly reveals the falsehoods upon which past beliefs have been based.

But there are some who are afraid of the police for other reasons, such as those which have deep-rooted origins in one's childhood or upbringing. Sometimes a belief imposed upon a child's mind will never be eradicated. A lot of children grow up in fear of the police because their parents have regularly threatened to 'tell the policeman' if they are naughty. And, for a child, it is naughty to spill one's dinner or wet one's pants. I believe children should be brought up with a healthy respect for the police, because the service exists for the benefit of all society and not just a portion of it, but I do not believe youngsters should be taught to fear the office of constable.

Having said that, there are those who nurse an irrational fear of the police, and over the years while patrolling from Aidensfield, I came to know such a woman in Ashfordly. The strange thing was that she was not frightened of *policemen* – she was frightened of police *stations*. Maybe she was a member of that group of people who fear or hate official places such as banks, dentists' surgeries, council chambers, income tax offices or DHSS departments. Whatever the root cause of her fear, she knew it was irrational and even silly, and yet she could do nothing to overcome it. She had no fear of police officers, however, and was quite happy to chat with them in the street or mingle with them socially. I grew to know her from my irregular but frequent patrols in Ashfordly, our local market town.

Being the village constable of Aidensfield, I had to patrol Ashfordly's streets from time to time, usually twice a week during a selected morning or afternoon, each time being a four-hour stint. We rural constables undertook such duties when the town was short of officers due to other commitments, such as court appearances, courses, annual leave and so on, and in time I came to know several Ashfordly residents.

One of them was a busy little woman who seemed to trot everywhere. She was in her middle forties, I estimated, with rimless spectacles and a hair-do that kept her dark brown locks firmly in place. She was always smartly dressed but she scarcely reached five feet in height. She had the tiniest of features – little feet, little hands, a little body, and she drove a little car, a Morris Mini, in fact. She was like a petite and pretty china doll and at times looked almost as fragile.

I first became aware of her as I patrolled the market-place. Periodically during the day she would rush in, park her tiny car and then trot into a succession of shops, offices and cottages, her tiny feet twinkling across the cobbles. Occasionally the face of a Yorkshire terrier would peer from the rear seat of her car, and sometimes there would be a poodle or a tiny terrier of some sort. More often that not, she was accompanied by a small dog, and if I was hovering anywhere nearby, she would smile and bid me good morning or good afternoon before rushing about her business.

There was no official reason for me to wonder who she was or what she was doing, but it is a feature of police work that one acquires local knowledge, often without realizing. And in time I learned that this was Mrs Delia Ballentine. She lived near the castle, and her husband, Geoff, worked for an agricultural implements dealer in Ashfordly. She did not have a job, but she was heavily engaged in work for local charities and organizations – she was secretary of the Ashfordly WI, for example, and she did voluntary work for the Red Cross, the parish church, the RSPCA and a host of other groups, which explained why she was always rushing.

The first time we spoke was when she was collecting for the Spastics Society. I was in the market-place in uniform when she asked if I'd care to make a donation, I did and was rewarded with a badge which I pinned to my tunic. I commented on the state of the weather, as English folk tend to do, and she said she had to hurry home to prepare Geoff's dinner, as Yorkshire people call their lunch. On several occasions thereafter she persuaded me to part with small sums of money for an amazing variety of charities and worthwhile causes, and in every case she had to rush off to attend to some other task.

Then one Friday morning, when the market was a riot of colour with its fascinating range of stalls, vehicles and crowds, I saw her collecting for a local school for handicapped children.

I slipped some money into her collecting box and said, 'You should get around to the police station. There's a conference there; it starts in twenty minutes. There's eight traffic officers just dying to support worthy causes. You might get a few bob, with a bit of luck.'

She shuddered. It was a visible shudder, and it surprised me. 'Oh, no.' She tried to shrug off the moment. 'I couldn't.'

'They wouldn't mind . . .' I began.

'No, it's not that.' She hesitated and I waited for her to continue. She added, 'I'm terrified of police stations.'

'Police stations?' I must have sounded sceptical, because she laughed at me.

'Silly, isn't it?' she chuckled at her own absurdity. 'I just don't like going inside police stations. I don't know why.'

'I can understand folks not wanting to go into a prison or even a lift, but I've never come across this before,' I said. 'But you're not frightened of policemen?'

'No, not at all,' she told me. 'That makes it all the dafter, doesn't it?'

'Well, if you ever go around to our station and I'm there, just shout and I'll come outside to see what you want!'

'Thanks, I will! Well, I must be off. I've other calls to make . . .' and she twinkled away towards her little car. A dachshund barked from the front passenger seat, and I wondered how many dogs she kept.

As she disappeared, I pondered upon her odd phobia and tried to work out whether there was a word for it. I knew that the fear of a particular place was known as topophobia, the fear of night was nyctophobia, and a fear of streets or crossing places was dromophobia. There were others, such as ergasiophobia, which is a fear of surgeries, brontophobia, which is a fear of thunder, and thalassophobia, which is a fear of the sea. A fear of confined spaces is claustrophobia, a fear of deep places is bathophobia, and a fear of dry places is xerophobia, with dipsophobia being a fear of drinking or drunkenness, and hydrophobia a fear of water or wet places. Thinking along these lines, I wondered if fear of police stations was nickophobia, cellophobia, custophobia or mere constabularophobia. Whatever its name, it was a curious and somewhat unsettling fear, but one with which she could live without too many problems. After all, many people live and die without ever entering a police station. I felt sure Delia could survive without having to face that challenge.

But I was wrong.

I was performing another tour of duty in Ashfordly one July afternoon and was in the police station when a youth came in. About seventeen years old, he was carrying a hessian sack which was dripping wet and squirming with some form of life.

'Now, what have got?' I asked him.

'Kittens,' he said. 'Somebody threw 'em into t'beck but they landed in some rushes, tied up in this sack. They didn't go right into t'water. I found 'em when I was fishing. They're all alive.'

He opened the top of the sack to reveal three beautiful black-and-white kittens, several weeks old. Their eyes were open and they were quite capable of walking. Within seconds, they were crawling all over the counter, and I asked him if he was prepared to keep them.

'No chance,' he said. 'I live with my granny, we've no space, that's why I fetched 'em here. I thought you'd know what to do.'

'Right, we'll see to them,' I assured him. 'Thanks for saving their lives. It was a rotten trick, eh? Throwing them in the beck like that.'

'If I'd seen who'd chucked 'em in, I'd have chucked him in an' all,' said the youth, whose name was Ian Trueman. I took details for our records, and off he went.

I was now left with the problem of three active and interesting kittens which had to be fed and housed, but we did have procedures for dealing with stray dogs and lost and found pets of every kind. Because these three active chaps were literally crawling into everything, threatening to overturn filing trays, clog the typewriter and send the telephone crashing to the floor, I decided to pop them into No. 2 cell until I could deal with them. A dish of milk would keep them happy as they explored its delights.

I began to prepare the cell for their stay. I went into the garage to find a cat tray and some litter or earth, found a saucer in the sergeant's office and used some of my own milk from a bottle I carried for my break periods. As I fussed over the kittens in their prison-like home, I heard someone enter the enquiry office, and so I called 'I won't be a moment'. I then tried to close the cell door without the kittens rushing out at my heels, for one of them seemed determined to escape from custody. I had to sit him on the cell bed as I rushed out. But in time I got them all safely behind the proverbial bars and returned to the enquiry office to dispose of the wet and ruined sack.

And there, to my astonishment, was Delia Ballentine. She was standing at the counter, holding on to the front edge of the top surface as she shook with fear and anxiety. I could see the perspiration standing out on her brow and could appreciate the sheer willpower that had driven her to enter this feared place.

'Hello,' I said, with the sack dangling from my hand. She could not speak for a moment. 'Let's go outside,' I suggested.

She shook her head. 'No, I must try to beat this silly fear.'

'There's no need.' I threw the sack into the rubbish bin and said, 'Look, Mrs Ballentine, I'll see you out there. It's no problem . . .'

She did not reply but stood with her hands gripping the edge of the counter until her knuckles turned white. Then I could hear the kittens mewing pitifully . . . she heard them too.

'What's that?' she asked, the fear vanishing from her face in an instant as she concentrated upon the distinctive distress cries.

'There's three kittens in our cell,' and I explained how they came to be here.

'Oh, the poor things! Can I take them? I mean, if no one wants them . . .'

'That would solve a lot of our problems,' I said. 'If no one claims them, we'd have to find a good home or have them put to sleep,' I told her.

During this conversation, it was fascinating to notice the apparent evaporation of her fear, and she even followed me into the cell as I went to retrieve the kittens. When I gave them to her, she seemed to be totally in control, her entire concentration being upon the tiny animals. As she petted them, I searched under the counter and found a cardboard box big enough to accommodate all three. I sat the box on the counter as I talked to her. But as I tried to elicit the reason for her visit, those tremblings and overt nervous tics returned, all heralded by the perspiration on her face. I found myself admiring her courage in making such a determined effort to enter this dreaded building.

Once I had the kittens safely inside the box, I took her outside and placed them on the back seat of her car as I tried to interview her. Now free from her trauma, she told me she had just discovered she had lost a precious brooch. It was in the shape of a swan and was made of 22 carat gold; it was antique, a present from her husband's grandmother, and she felt she had to come to report it. Losing it had been of sufficient worry to compel her to overcome her resistance to police stations.

So I recorded particulars, saying that if it came to our notice, it would be restored to her. In fact, it was later returned to her, albeit not through our assistance – someone had found it in the back room of the town hall and had recognized it. Apparently, Delia had been to a WI meeting there a couple of days earlier and the brooch had become detached from her dress. She hailed me in the street shortly after its return; I said I was delighted and would delete it from our records.

'You didn't come to the station to report its recovery?' I asked, wondering if she had made such an attempt.

'No, I couldn't, I really couldn't. I thought because I'd done it once, I could do it again but I just couldn't, Mr Rhea. I really did try. That first time, I think I was so worried about what Geoff would say about my losing the brooch that I managed to force myself to go into the station.'

'But those cats, Mrs Ballentine, when you saw those kittens, you lost all your fears, if only for a few moments.'

'I know, and I thought I could do it again without the cats, but I couldn't. I know it's so silly, but it must be something deep inside that makes me frightened, mustn't it?'

'I'm no medical expert, but it does seem to be a psychological problem!' I smiled. 'Anyway, you've got your precious brooch back and I'm delighted. Now, those kittens? Did you get them a good home?'

'We're still looking after them, until they're a wee bit older, but I've got some people interested in them. Look, Mr Rhea, if ever you get any more kittens or other animals in, I'll take them off your hands. I'd rather do that than let you have them put down.'

'We'd welcome that sort of arrangement.' I was delighted to hear this. 'Found animals can be a problem to us. But you'd not be able to call and collect them?'

'You or your men would have to deliver them to the house or bring them out to the car, I'm afraid.' She looked slightly embarrassed at her own frailty.

'That is no problem,' I said. 'I'll have a word with Sergeant Bairstow or Sergeant Blaketon and see that your name goes in our records. I'm sure we can arrange a cat and mouse delivery service when it's necessary.'

And so it came to pass.

This explains why, from time to time in Ashfordly, a police van can be seen motoring through the town with passengers which vary from cats and dogs to budgerigars, parrots and canaries, via hamsters, pet mice, white rabbits and even iguanas or ferrets. In all cases, they showed far less fear of our police station and its cells than did Mrs Delia Ballentine.

While Delia Ballentine had a genuine fear of police stations, Daniel Joseph Price hated police officers. Indeed, he hated everything connected with the service – its uniform, its members, its offices and its duties. There was absolutely nothing he liked about us. He made no secret of this loathing. Whenever he spotted me, he would make a point of approaching me, vociferously to broadcast aspects of his lifelong hatred.

'I hate coppers,' he would say as he glared at me. 'I really do hate coppers. I'll never help the police, you know that? Never.'

When he first made this attitude known to me, I tried to elicit some reason for his hatred, but he would never explain. I tried asking other people, but they did not know either, and so the deep-seated cause of Daniel's continuing malice remained a mystery. In time, I grew to accept his verbal outbursts, whether in the street or in the pub, and I didn't feel too concerned about his attitude. After a while, I never tried to reason with him or to make any response.

Following months of listening to him, I adopted a new tactic. Whenever he approached me to announce his persistent hatred, I would simply say, 'Thanks, Dan, I know. You've told me many times.'

But this served only to compel him to emphasize his vitriol. 'But I really do hate policemen, Mr Rhea. Do you understand what I'm saying?'

'Yes, I do, and I accept it,' I would say, wondering whether he expected some kind of violent reaction or official response from me.

Once I said, 'If you hate policemen, it's your own problem, not mine. I can do nothing about it. If it's any consolation, I don't hate you. I don't hate anyone, Daniel. And if you were in trouble, I would help you, either when I'm off duty or on.'

'But I'll never help you, Mr Rhea. Can't you understand that? I'll never give you information about crimes, I'll never warn you of trouble, I'll never come to your help if you are in bother, I'll never be a witness for you . . .'

In an effort to create some kind of positive reply to his ramblings, I tried to explain that helping the police was not merely of benefit to the officers concerned – helping the police was a way of helping society. Police officers gained nothing from such aid, other than the satisfaction of helping the public to deal with wrongdoers, whether the wrongdoers were criminals or merely those in need of professional help. But Daniel could not see it in that way. He seemed to think that helping the police was against his religion or that there was something grossly anti-social in volunteering to provide information or assistance to us.

I did wonder to what extent he would continue his one-man campaign. I came to realize that he did not hate me in person; indeed, he would sometimes buy me a drink if I was off duty. The odd thing was that, while buying me the drink, he would announce that he really did hate policemen, although he had nothing against me personally.

This peculiar relationship endured for a long time, and I must admit I took little heed of his words. In some ways, I quite liked Daniel. He was honest, if nothing else, and he did spend a lot of time helping the old folk in Aidensfield, doing their shopping for them or bits of decorating and cleaning. He had a wonderful manner with children too, being a bundle of fun during the village sports days, church fêtes and the like. He worked as a labourer on building sites, always managing to find local employment, and he lived with his mother in one of the council houses. He was never troublesome from my point of view, he never came rolling home drunk or abusive. He did not run a car but used an old black pedal cycle to get around the lanes. In his mid forties, he was a solidly built man who was a shade overweight, and his round, somewhat flabby face usually bore a contented smile. He did seem to be a very contented person – until he saw me.

During his leisure moments, he wore a well-tailored black suit. I never saw him in a sports jacket or casual wear of any kind; even when cycling to the pub or romping around at a garden fête, he would wear his black suit, and the result of this continual wear was that it had become extremely shabby. At close quarters, I could see that the suit was made of quality material, and sometimes I wondered whether he was descended from a sophisticated family who had fallen on hard times, the suit having perhaps belonged to some long-dead and wealthy male ancestor.

Alternatively, he might have bought it at a jumble sale. It was certainly from a bygone era. When new, it would have been beyond his financial limits and perhaps his social horizons, but it never seemed to wear out and was an undoubted bargain. I'm sure he regarded it as a worthwhile acquisition, and I'm equally sure he cherished it, but a visit to the cleaners would have worked miracles.

In my daily patrols, I had a feeling that, sooner or later in my professional life, I would encounter Daniel's bigotry. It was almost inevitable in a village the size of Aidensfield, where one's neighbours and fellow residents live so close to each other. From time to time, I tried to anticipate the kind of problems it would present, and then I endeavoured to work out a series of feasible responses. And, sure enough, that day did arrive – but it brought a curious problem that I had not foreseen.

At five o'clock one evening, which was in fact my day off, there was a knock at the door, and I opened it to find Daniel standing there in his crumpled, greasy suit. He looked far from happy, and I realized that something pretty awful must have happened to persuade him to call voluntarily at the police house.

'Come in, Daniel.' I stood back and held open the door.

'No,' he said. 'I'll say my piece here.'

'As you wish.' I had no intention of antagonizing him.

'Somebody's pinched our silver tray!' He rushed out the words as if he was talking treason. 'T'insurance man says I've got to tell t'police, so I'm telling you.'

'I'll have to take details,' I began. 'You are reporting a crime to me.'

'T'insurance said I had to tell t'police. I've told you, so that's it.'

'No, it isn't it,' I said. 'It's not as simple as that, Daniel. I've got official forms to compile if you are reporting a crime. The insurance will expect a full report from us, and I can't do that without doing my job properly. So either you come in and help me fill in those forms, or I will not be able to complete the necessary details.'

He stared at his feet for a few moments, and I knew he was wrestling with his conscience. I made no comment about his previous antagonism and simply waited with the door held open. With a massive sigh, he stepped over the threshold, and I led him into my office. I must admit I experienced a feeling of success. I seated him beside the desk, drew the necessary crime report forms from the drawer and explained the formalities involved. But he was most reluctant to provide me with all the facts; he saw this as helping the police. In carrying out this interview, I had to drag every piece of information from him.

Through persistent questioning, I did learn that two men had visited his mother that morning, ostensibly to see if she had any old junk or ornaments to sell. They had told a good story and, while one had kept her talking, the other had explored the house. Only after they'd gone had the old lady realized the tray was missing. Daniel was clearly upset, especially at the evil way his elderly mother had been treated by these rogues.

I could see that he was battling with his conscience – he wanted the tray found and the rogues caught, but he did not want to break his lifelong embargo by helping the police. As a consequence, I did succeed in abstracting sufficient information for completion of my official form but not enough upon which to base a thorough investigation. For example, he would not or could not give me a detailed description of the missing tray, save to say it was roughly oval in shape with a handle at each end and legs underneath. It was a large one, some two feet long by twelve inches wide. It sounded more like a piece of silverware from a stately home than a tray from a Yorkshire council house. He offered no description of the two men, nor did he provide me with any of the *modus operandi* they had utilized.

I decided I would have to talk to Mrs Price but made a mental note to do so tomorrow – and then a thought struck me. Daniel would not have come to seek my official help without some kind of pressure, so did this tray belong to him or his mother? I had assumed it was his property, but now I began to suspect it was very important to her and that that could be the reason for his uncharacteristic visit. I became even more determined to talk to her and would do so when Daniel was at work. In the meantime, I could enter the crime into the official channels with an assurance that further enquiries would be made. Having made this uncharacteristic visit, Daniel rushed away.

At ten o'clock next morning, I paid a visit to Mrs Price and found her at home and quite composed. She was slightly stooped with age, but her hair still bore signs of its original auburn, and her brown eyes were alert and full of life. Upon recognizing me, she bade me enter her smart, clean home and settled me on the settee, insisting that I have a cup of tea.

'I've come about the missing tray, Mrs Price,' I said.

'Daniel did not want to bother you,' she smiled, 'but I insisted. The insurance company said it must be reported stolen, you see, but, well, Daniel is a bit silly when it comes to dealing with policemen.'

'I need a detailed description of the tray, Mrs Price, one that we can circulate among antique-dealers and salerooms.'

'Oh, Daniel said it would not be necessary. He said you'd never do anything to trace it, you'd just record it so the insurance company could be sure it was a crime.'

'Then Daniel is wrong, Mrs Price. We will circulate a full description to every police force in the United Kingdom, to Interpol and to all antique-dealers, salerooms, silversmiths and others who might be offered it. And, of course, our CID will make local enquiries about the men who took it.'

'Then a photograph would be useful?' she smiled. I found her to be an amazingly alert and wise old woman, with a keen brain and a wry sense of humour.

'It would be ideal.'

'Then I have one or two.'

She ferreted about in a cupboard near the fireplace and produced an old leather-bound album which she opened. Inside were lots of old prints, some secured in the book and others loosely assembled. But in time her bent old fingers found the ones she sought, and she passed them to me. I found myself looking at a silver salver. It was exquisitely ornate and bore a coat of arms in the centre.

'Daniel could not put a value upon it, Mrs Price,' I told her, 'but this seems to be a very valuable piece of silver.'

'It is, Mr Rhea, in terms of both money and sentimentality. Now Daniel could not put a value upon it simply because I have never given him any idea of its worth.'

'I put it down as £10,' I confessed to her.

'I'd put it much closer to twenty times that, Mr Rhea. Now listen. When Daniel was a youth, he was rather impetuous and liable to do silly things, and so I have never revealed the full nature of that salver to him. He knew it was a family heirloom but thought it was just an old tray I had inherited. In fact, it is the only thing I have which can be traced through my family – the tray was made in 1779; it bears that date. The coat of arms is my family crest.'

I did not ask about the circumstances of the family, but she did say her grandfather had tried to sell the family silver, hence the photographs were intended for the catalogue, but her own mother had rescued this salver. It had been withdrawn and given to her mother, and now it was hers; when she died, it should have passed to Daniel. She had sent Daniel to report the theft, not realizing how much detail I would require and not appreciating his own lack of knowledge of what should have been a fascinating inheritance. My mind now flashed to the old suit that Daniel habitually wore – had that also come from grandad? It seemed that Daniel was of noble ancestry, but just how far back in history I could not guess. It might be a subject for some genealogical research – even by Daniel, if he so wished.

Thanks to my visit and the alertness of Mrs Price, I did walk away with a detailed description of the salver, a far better idea of its value and a very useful photograph. I also managed to obtain reasonable descriptions of the two thieves – apparently, one of them had said he'd like to go to the toilet, and she'd allowed him upstairs to the bathroom. The salver had been kept on a dressing-table in the spare bedroom – the thief had seen it and had somehow smuggled it out of the house, probably stuffed up his jacket. Nothing else was missing.

When I informed Detective Sergeant Gerry Connolly, he was pleased the matter had been recorded – and he was delighted with the photograph. He told me that in recent weeks a team of two supposed antique-dealers had been operating in the area, and Mrs Price had been their most recent victim. Their MO was simple: they entered houses occupied by elderly folks under the pretext of inspecting and valuing goods, and while one kept the householder occupied, the other would find an excuse for exploring the house. They removed anything that took their fancy. And now, thanks to her, a fairly comprehensive description of the men was available – she had been able to fill gaps left by other old folks. But, more important to the Prices, the salver was identifiable. The coat of arms in the centre made it unique, and so copies of the photo were made for the widest possible distribution.

Two nights later I popped into the Brewers Arms at Aidensfield while on a late evening patrol and saw Daniel in his usual corner at the bar. He saw me, smiled briefly and nodded, but on this occasion there was no bravado about his refusing to co-operate with the police. I did not mention the theft before his pals – if he wished to do so, that was his privilege, and after checking the ages of some youngsters in the lounge, I left.

It was five days later when I got a call from Detective Sergeant Connolly.

'Ah, Nick, glad to have caught you. We've some good news – that silver salver of Mrs Price's. It's been recovered.'

'Really? Where?' I was delighted, more for Mrs Price than for myself.

'Birmingham. Birmingham City Police have done wonders for us – they've set up an Antiques Squad, and one of their lads spotted the salver in an antique shop. The dealer paid £850 for it – so whoever sold it to him knew it was worth a bob or two. But the even better news is that it has a set of fingerprints on it, and we're hoping they match those of our suspects. That'll take a day or two.'

'So when can Mrs Price have it back?' I asked.

'It'll take a while. If we get the villains, we'll need the salver for evidence, so we're talking of a couple of months or so at the least. But at least it's safe, and she will get it back eventually.'

'Thanks, Sergeant, that's great news. I'll go and tell her.'

But when I knocked on the door, Daniel opened it.

'What do you want?' he asked bluntly.

'I'd like to talk to your mother,' I said.

'Mother? What for?'

'About the stolen salver. I understand it is her property, Daniel, not yours.'

His face showed I had scored a point over him. Then Mrs Price came to see who was at the door and beckoned me to enter. 'Come in, Mr Rhea.'

With Daniel following me into the front room, she showed me the settee and smiled. 'Well, Mr Rhea, you have some news?'

'Yes.' I was so pleased for her as I explained the developments. Daniel listened too, but when I'd finished, he said, 'You mean you came here to quiz my mother after I'd given you all that help?'

'There were certain things to clarify, Daniel, and a more detailed description to obtain; you were at work. Your mother was most helpful . . .'

'I didn't tell you of Mr Rhea's visit, Daniel, because I knew how you'd react, you silly man. Anyway, it has paid dividends – the salver is safe again. Safe for you, I might add, although I'm not sure that you deserve it!'

'But I gave all the information to him, then he comes sneaking into my house asking question, snooping behind my back, poking his nose into my private life . . .'

'Daniel!' said Mrs Price. 'You are a silly fool.'

'I'll go.' I stood up to leave. 'I'll be in touch when we've more news, Mrs Price.'

'I hate the police,' said Daniel, standing up to follow me to the door. 'They're so untrustworthy, so devious . . .'

Mrs Price just smiled.

7 *Private Lives*

> The only trouble is, we do not understand what is happening to our neighbours.
>
> Joseph Chamberlain (1836–1914)

Each of us feels entitled to a private life in which we may do as we please within the confines of our own home. If that statement sounds eminently just, the reality is not quite like that, because our private life and behaviour are regulated. For example, we must be careful not to disturb or upset the neighbours in a way that infringes the law.

The truth is that we cannot do exactly as we wish, even within our own home. Instead, there are many rules to restrict the use to which we can put our home. For example, it cannot legally become a brothel or a place for taking drugs, nor can it become a slaughter-house, public house, pawnbroker's shop, firearms dealer's premises, nursing home, gaming house, pet shop, theatre or hotel without some official intervention. Furthermore, we cannot do exactly as we wish within our own home, because we might antagonize one of the many official agencies. Running a scrap-metal business from the back yard, a horse-racing establishment from the front lawn, a cats' home in the garden shed, or rock concerts in the attic might not receive universal approval.

In spite of many restrictions, though, it may still be said that an Englishman's home is his castle, because we can enjoy a high degree of privacy within its confines. This reassuring old saying comes from the famous lawyer, statesman and jurist Sir Edward Coke (1552–1634): 'The house of everyone is to him as his castle and fortress, as well for his defence against injury or violence as for his repose.' The trouble with most of us is that we respect that notion up to a point, for, if we are honest, we still like to know what the neighbours are doing, and then we might object if their behaviour annoys us.

The snag is that the actions of one's neighbours can often extend beyond the immediate boundaries of their home, at times affecting the entire community. Simple and acceptable examples might include weddings and funerals which, although based on one's home, do in varying degrees affect the state of prevailing calm in a village community. Lots of people arrive, traffic is generated, crowds of spectators assemble, curiosity is aroused and the movement of ordinary people is sometimes restricted to permit the procession to pass. We do not object to that, nor do we normally object when something other than a wedding or funeral occurs, particularly when there is a positive increase in the interest shown by a healthy community.

Examples in Aidensfield included a visit by Her Majesty The Queen to nearby Hovingham on the occasion of the wedding of the Duke and Duchess of Kent, the visit of Sophia Loren to Castle Howard, along with Peter Ustinov and other famous faces, while filming *Lady L*, followed by several other camera crews who came later to film sequences for James Herriot's books.

During my constableship, Aidensfield itself was host to a surprising number of very famous people, ranging from British prime ministers to one of Charlie Chaplin's daughters, via cousins of the American president and several foreign princes and princesses. All were highly identifiable in a village of fewer than 200 souls. Nonetheless, in the midst of all this excitement, the village people afforded these guests a welcome degree of privacy. Word of their presence rarely reached anyone outside the community, the press never got to hear of their visits, and these famous folk could pop into the Brewers Arms or walk across the local moors without fear of being accosted by admirers, photographers and hangers-on.

As the village constable, I was often privy to these occasions, being asked by the hosts to ward off any unwelcome attention should it arise. I think it is fair to say that the people of Aidensfield became accustomed to having the famous and wealthy as guests in their pretty village.

Their discretion and loyalty to such a visitor were tested during one long, hot summer.

The story, which involves the private lives to two people, centres upon the old blacksmith's workshop. When the last blacksmith of Aidensfield ended his craft, an enterprising young man called Kevin Bell purchased the premises and turned it into a craftsman woodworker's shop. He began to produce handmade goods of every kind, from large items of furniture to such small objects as serviette rings, ashtrays, egg cups and three-legged stools.

Like so many local woodworkers, he carved an emblem upon his work. Hereabouts we have the Mouseman of Kilburn who carves everything in oak and then adorns it with his famous mouse trademark; there are those who identify their handicraft with acorns, lizards, owls and other distinctive marks. Kevin chose his own name for his logo and carved a bell upon his products. His work was good, his furniture was sound, and his application implied a determination to succeed. And so he did. He would never become a millionaire but he would and did become a respected craftsman.

But there was a mystery about Kevin.

He came to live and work in Aidensfield some months after my own arrival, but he was not a local man. He came from York, having nurtured a dream of becoming a rural craftsman, and I respected him for having the nerve to put his ambition to the test. He was a tall man, around thirty years old, with a slightly balding head of light brown hair; slim and powerful, he played cricket and squash.

Everyone liked Kevin – he became a welcome and important asset to Aidensfield. He made his home in the limestone cottage adjoining the old blacksmith's shop. This had been the home of a succession of blacksmiths, many of whom had been content to live in rather primitive conditions, but Kevin's woodworking skills and DIY ability turned it into a dream house.

The mystery which puzzled the local people involved his family.

An older woman came to live there, a Mrs Marie Bell, and we discovered she was Kevin's mother. She was in her mid fifties, we estimated, for her blonde hair was turning grey. She became a part of the village community by joining the Women's Institute and helping with parish church matters. In time, I learned that her husband had died, and so she had come to live with her unmarried son in Aidensfield. The arrangement seemed a good one, for it meant that Kevin had someone to look after his precious house, to ensure he was adequately fed and his clothes were washed. Mum and son appeared to have none of the problems that can accrue when different generations live together.

There was also a small boy, about seven years old. He came at the same time as Mrs Bell and was called Robert. As he was of a build and colouring similar to Kevin's, everyone assumed he was a late arrival in the family. Without asking or prying, they assumed that Mrs Bell had produced him just prior to her menopause, a time when many women are likely to conceive. The Bells did nothing to change that assumption.

Young Robert joined the local school, accompanied Mrs Bell to the shop or upon bus rides in Ashfordly, went to other children's houses for parties and invited them back, and took part in most of the village's events. Everyone called him Robert Bell, he called Mrs Bell 'mummy', and he related to Kevin as if the latter was an elder brother.

But I was to learn the truth.

As with so many of these family secrets, the truth came out quite accidentally and, having learned it in that way, I had no intention of making anyone else aware of young Robert's ancestry. The names I am now using are, of course, not the family's real ones, but I have been allowed to reveal that secret in this book – not that it is of earth-shattering consequence.

It seemed that some years earlier Kevin and a girl called Teresa Craven had had a long and enjoyable relationship whose result was Robert. Because Teresa had been eighteen at the time and on the threshold of a major career, Kevin said he would bring up the boy in the hope that perhaps she would one day marry him and settle down to motherhood. The caring Kevin had no wish to prevent Teresa's following her career – it was a most noble gesture, I felt. Then, when Kevin's father died, Mrs Bell took over the responsibility for the little lad;

it was a voluntary offer from a family which, I had already learned, was thoroughly nice and decent.

A bonus was that Teresa was now making a name in her chosen career, and she did visit her son from time to time. And she remained on good terms with Kevin – he seemed quite content to give her all the freedom she desired until she decided to settle down, marry him and raise their son.

This gem of local knowledge came to me through a colleague who served in York City Police. I learned this piece of news when he and I performed duty together at York Races – officers from the North Riding of Yorkshire were drafted in to perform duty at the races, and I found myself working with Tim Lewis. We chatted and he told me that a friend of his had moved to Aidensfield – that friend was Kevin Bell. And so, in this manner, I learned something of Kevin's past. It was during this chat that Tim told me about Teresa's career.

'Does the name Terry Craven mean anything to you?' he asked.

'No,' I admitted. 'Should it?'

'Not unless you're a tennis buff,' he said. 'She's our great white hope for Wimbledon.'

'Oh, *that* Terry Craven!' I had heard the name; in fact, she had been featured only recently in the national newspapers.

Tim went on to say she had been born in York but had moved away with her parents, returning from time to time to visit relatives. She was a talented and highly promising tennis player and had been offered a scholarship at an American university. There she would be coached in the very best of techniques by some of the world's finest exponents. Shortly before going to the USA she had come to York for a holiday, where she had met Kevin and become pregnant. And, Kevin being Kevin, he had promised to bring up the child so that Teresa could follow her career.

In my time at Aidensfield, she had completed her American course and was now part of the world tennis circuit, playing in tournaments at all the major venues – and she was winning. She was high in the list of British seeded women players, being one of our top exponents. From my friend Tim, I understood that when her tennis career was over and her world tours ended, she would marry Kevin and settle down to being a mum for Robert. It was a remarkable tale.

Terry did visit Aidensfield on a regular basis. When her hectic lifestyle permitted her to take time off, she would come to stay quietly in Aidensfield. She stayed with Kevin and his mother and would go for long walks with young Robert. I think he thought she was an aunt – certainly, the other children referred to her as 'Aunt Teresa'. I'm sure most of the village thought so too, although I suspect many did realize the true relationships within that happy family. Her other role, as a leading British ladies tennis-player, was hardly mentioned; those who did not follow tennis would never know of her, for she had not yet become what is termed a 'household name', nor was she universally recognized in airports and public places.

Then things began to go wrong.

I was in the bar of the Brewers Arms one Friday lunchtime in early May, making one of my routine uniformed visits, when a long-haired young man burst in. He rushed across to the bar, ordered a pint and started to chatter to the locals. He sat at one of the tables with some regulars and bought them all a drink, a bonus to their usual lunchtime pint. At first I paid no heed to his behaviour, thinking it was someone known to these characters. Then he came over to me.

'Ah, the village constable, the fountain of all knowledge, the man with everyone's secret tucked in his notebook. Constable,' he smiled at me, 'can I get you a drink?'

'No thanks. I'm on duty,' I said.

'Well, you might be able to help me. The name's Craig.' And he said he was a reporter for one of the less savoury of the Sunday national newspapers. As he talked, I caught the eye of one of the men at the table he'd just left – the man shook his head slowly from side to side. I knew they had not co-operated.

'It depends,' I said cautiously. 'If it's anything to do with the force, we do have an official spokesman.'

'It's nothing to do with the force, Constable,' he said, sipping his pint. 'It's local knowledge I'm after. You'll know of Terry Craven?' I shook my head. 'But you must, the tennis player . . . the next great British Wimbledon champion . . .'

'Sorry, I don't follow tennis.' I pretended to be ignorant. 'I've never heard of him.'

'Look, you can't be much of a village guardian if you don't know her; it's not a him, it's a her, Terry as in Teresa, not Terence. She comes here a lot. Stays in the village, according to my sources . . .'

'Really? We get lots of very famous people here,' I said. 'A tennis-player doesn't make a lot of impact, I'm afraid. Are you sure you haven't got this village confused with Aidensford in Surrey? Some do, you know.'

'No, I have not. Aidensfield is the place. She comes here for quiet holidays. Somebody must know her . . . it's the tiniest bloody village I've ever been in . . . everybody must know everybody else's business . . .'

'If they do know, they respect each other,' I said. 'Now, do you lads know her?' I asked the men at the table and also the barman whose name was Sid. They all shook their heads and muttered their denials. It was a convincing act on their part.

'Why do you want to know?' I asked.

'There's a tale doing the rounds saying she's got a bairn, an illegitimate kid, farmed out. I'm onto the story, I'm after an exclusive . . .'

'You've got the wrong spot here, mate,' said Sid. 'As Mr Rhea says, you must be thinking of Aidensford down south.'

It was evident that the reporter realized there was a conspiracy of silence, and he stormed out. The moment he'd gone, Sid put into operation the unofficial but highly effective Early Warning System we had created. This served all the businesses in the village and surrounding areas. If one received a visit from, say, a con man or someone trying to pass dud cheques, that business would ring another three, who in turn would ring another three and so on, thus warning everyone within a very short time. This useful system was now being operated for the benefit of Teresa Craven.

'Thanks, Sid,' I said. 'I'll go and warn Kevin and Mrs Bell.'

'That bastard! Why do those bloody awful Sunday papers dig up dirt like that? And who buys them anyway?'

As I warned a grateful Kevin of the man's visit, so Sid's system alerted the other places of public resort in Aidensfield and beyond. I was to learn later that the reporter had received absolutely no information from the village, and I was pleased, if only that young Robert's life was being protected from sensational and scandalous journalism.

But it did not end there. On the following Sunday the pub was inundated with journalists – all the muckraking papers were represented and there were a few reputable ones there too. News of a possible indiscretion in Terry Craven's life had permeated the newsrooms and canteens of many papers.

The heavy-spending reporters were buying drinks for all the regulars, hoping that tongues would be freed and news would flow. But Sid had done his duty. No one was prepared to speak, and young Robert's 'Bell' surname and his home at the blacksmith's shop saved his family from investigation. More drink was purchased and more questions were asked, but no answers were given.

Then, without warning to anyone, the local ne'er-do-well, who had the curious name of Claude Jeremiah Greengrass, came into the Brewers Arms. This was not his usual pub – he tended to haunt the Hopbind Inn at Elsinby – but he must have sensed that something important was happening in Aidensfield and that free drinks were available, along with the chance to earn a few bob. He had turned up like the proverbial bad penny. Claude was a pest. Small, pinched and totally untrustworthy, he was always in trouble of some kind; his offences were usually of a minor nature and he lived on his wits. As he materialized in that bar, I scented danger. He was the one man who might reveal the truth, and the others were not in a fit state to warn him by now. They could hardly talk – the reporters had virtually defeated themselves in getting everyone paralytic. But I knew that Claude would know Terry's secret – he knew everyone's secrets . . .

'Ah!' A *News of the World* reporter spotted him before I could reach him through the crowd. 'A newcomer! You, here! Can I get you a drink?'

'I allus has a rum before my Sunday dinner.' He beamed at the journalist, his wizened face crinkling in a leathery smile.

A rum was duly bought.

'Claude,' I said. 'I'd like a word . . .'

'Later, Mr Rhea, I've got drink in my hand, and I never interrupts that, not for you, nor for anybody.'

'But before you talk to these men . . .'

'What men?' asked Claude, and he winked at me. I knew what he meant. He sipped his first rum, savouring the taste as the journalist waited. I left him with the journalist.

'Er, what's your name?'

'Greengrass.'

'Mr Greengrass, we are interested in a young lady called Craven . . .'

'My glass is empty. I allus likes a rum before my Sunday dinner,' said Claude, and I watched the twinkle in his eye. His glass was refilled, and he sipped it slowly. When it was empty, the journalist began, 'Mr Greengrass . . .'

'I do like a rum before my Sunday dinner,' repeated Claude.

The regulars lost count of Claude Jeremiah's rums, because they had also lost count of their own beers, whiskies and brandies. The outcome of that visit by the press was heavy expenditure for the press, a hefty Sunday lunchtime trading session by the Brewers Arms, a lot of late meals in the farms and cottages of the area, and several thumping headaches.

But no one revealed any information about Terry. The reporters had wasted a fortune. Afterwards I thanked Claude Jeremiah.

'It's not often I congratulate you,' I said, 'but you did real well.'

'I do like a rum before my Sunday dinner, Mr Rhea, so when I heard about Terry and that the press were there doling out free booze, I thought they owed me drink or two. I mean to say, they've printed enough scandalous tales about me.'

And so they had. He'd earned his rums.

I think that incident convinced the gutter press that they'd never succeed in getting a story of Terry Craven's private life from the villagers of Aidensfield. The people had, without exception, closed ranks to protect her and her child. I was proud of them.

But the story did not end there. That year, Terry reached the quarter-finals before being knocked out of Wimbledon.

We were all proud of her. In the autumn she returned to Aidensfield for a few weeks rest. She had been told of the village's response to the press enquiries and, in her gratitude, decided to throw a party for everyone in the Brewers Arms. She would pay for all the drinks and a buffet supper. I went along with Mary, for I was off duty, and it was a wonderful occasion. Even Claude Jeremiah had been invited. Everyone was happy for Terry and very proud of her achievements as they sang and drank her health. She made a little speech too. She said that, once her tennis-playing days were over, she would come to live permanently in Aidensfield with her son and husband. She told us that, in fact, she and Kevin were engaged to be married – that was another secret which no one knew.

Five or six years later, she did return and now lives happily in the area as Mrs Kevin Bell. She never won Wimbledon, but she did once reach the semi-finals.

But even now, if you enter the Brewers Arms on a Sunday lunchtime, you might encounter an elf-like man with a wizened and sun-tanned face. If you are unwise enough to ask him a question, it could become an expensive exercise, because, with expectation in his voice, he will respond with, 'I do enjoy a rum before my Sunday dinner.'

Some older maps of the North York Moors show an isolated house known as Owlet Hall. But a search will fail to locate it, because it no longer stands proud in its moorland setting. Sadly, it was demolished, and this is the story.

For many generations, it had been occupied by the Barr family, the last being Jason and Sarah Barr. They had scraped a tough living from the surrounding moorland, chiefly by farming sheep, and they had eked out their existence by undertaking other jobs. They would help their neighbours at harvest, for example, or give assistance at sheep sales, fairs and haytime.

Jason and Sarah had one son called William. He was himself retired, an ex-farmworker, and lived quietly in a council house at Aidensfield. Born at Owlet Hall, he had left the lonely spot in his teens to seek work in the dales, recognizing that his primitive family home, which boasted no water, drains or electricity, could never support him or any family. His parents had lived there until shortly before their deaths, when the house had passed to him. But there was nothing he could do with it. To bring it up to modern standards would have cost him more money than he had earned in a lifetime. No one wanted to buy it, due to its remote position and increasingly dilapidated condition, and no one seemed willing to undertake the expense of 'doing it up'.

The result was that the once-proud house was allowed to fall down, piece by piece. The woodwork of the windows was rotting, parts of the roof were collapsing, and when the back door rotted from its hinges, the ground floor became a shelter for sheep, moorland birds and the occasional hiker. However, upon my appointment as village constable at Aidensfield, the house was still standing and, in spite of its condition, was remarkably dry and cosy inside. It had been built to withstand the rigours of the moorland weather, and I always felt it looked charming in its patch of green. I often wished I had had the enormous sums necessary to renovate it.

Then one day, as I was patrolling the lonely road which ran past Owlet Hall, I noticed a couple of old cars parked outside. They were battered and rusting and painted in what became known as psychedelic colours, all a jumble of bright reds, oranges, blacks, blues, greens and more besides. I parked my van on the moor and walked over to them. Neither was taxed, I noted, but as they were not on public roads, I could not instigate proceedings. Then a long-haired youth with a colourful band around his head and small rimless glasses perched on the end of his nose appeared at the broken door.

'Want something?' he asked.

'I'm checking these cars,' I said. 'Are they yours?'

'They are,' and he offered no more information.

'They're not taxed.' I had to make the point.

'They're not on the road,' he said.

'But if they do go on the road, you'll make sure they are taxed and insured?' He just smiled, a gentle but cheeky smile. 'I'll be watching for them,' I said, smiling back at him. 'Are you staying long?'

'As long as need be,' he said. 'There's eight of us. We're no trouble, we just want to live our lives as we want, with no hassle, no authoritarian oppression, no rules, just happiness and freedom . . .'

'Flower power, communal living and free love?' I had heard these phrases in recent months and had seen reports about the people who had adopted these new ideals. They were hippies.

'That's about it,' he said.

'You've got permission to live here?' I asked.

'No, but we don't need it. We're squatting. We can squat in empty houses and no one can throw us out. I'm sure you know that,' he smiled. 'Besides, this old spot is derelict, falling down, full of holes and no doors. We'll fix it for ourselves.'

I stayed a few moments chatting to this man without seeing any of his friends, and decided they were harmless out here. Indeed, they might make some repairs to William's old house.

It was a further two or three days before I came across William Barr. He was collecting his pension from the post office/shop at Aidensfield and I took the opportunity to chat to him.

'Bill,' I said, 'that old house of yours, Owlet Hall. I was driving past earlier this week and see you've got visitors. A bunch of flower-power people, by the look of it. Your old home's been turned into a hippie commune.'

I explained what I had seen, and he thought for a while.

'They'll not be harming anybody?' he said.

'No, I think not,' I had to admit. 'They're supposed to be a friendly lot, a bit weird by our standards, but they're not likely to plan bank raids or kill moorland sheep for meat.'

'Then they can stay,' he said. 'T'awd spot might as well be useful to somebody.'

And so he allowed them to remain. In fact, it wouldn't have been easy get rid of them for, if pressed, they would surely claim squatters' rights, but because I was aware of their presence, I recorded the matter in my files.

I told the CID, with a special note to the Drugs Squad, for it was known that similar communes had cultivated cannabis plants, and I made a mental note to call at the house every three months or so, with a view to enforcing whichever of our laws they might be breaking. I would let them know of my continuing official interest, for I had no wish for the local youngsters to experiment with drugs of any kind.

By the time of my next visit, things had changed. The old cars were still there, still untaxed and still in their gaudy colours, but there was much more. That extra stuff was rubbish. It was everywhere. The exterior of the hitherto tidy old house was cluttered with every conceivable item of junk – old prams, bedsteads, chairs, a rusty oven, bikes, bottles, lengths of timber, flower pots – it looked like an itinerant trader's encampment of the very worst kind. I picked my way through the miasma to peep at the cars, and the man I'd first met appeared once again.

'Hi, Constable,' he beamed. 'You're back.'

'Yes, and I'll keep coming. This is part of my patch.'

'We're not criminals, man, we're friends to everyone.'

'Is this rubbish all yours?'

'Sure. The council doesn't collect it, so it stays.'

'You might try to remove it, or even burn some.'

'No hassle, man, no hassle. It's ours; we'll deal with it if we want; if we don't want, we won't. So who cares?'

'The people who live round here don't like their area looking like a council tip,' I said. 'They're proud of their countryside and don't like it to be desecrated.'

'Dr Johnson said that fine clothes are good only as they supply the want of other means of procuring respect,' said the fellow. 'External appearances don't matter. It's the soul that matters, man. So what's a bit of rubbish? Superficial, that's all. Unimportant in the real world . . .'

'You should try to keep the place neat, tidy and clean,' I tried again.

'Why, Constable, why? To get respect? False respect? People must take us as we are or not at all. Why pretend? We mean no harm, we just want to live our lives in peace.'

'And so do the villagers,' I said. 'Their rights and opinions are as valid as yours.'

'Sure they are.' He beamed and vanished indoors.

I was powerless to prosecute them under the Litter Act, because this was not a public place – it was private land. And the Civic Amenities Act was not then in force.

Over the following months, the hippies made themselves increasingly unwelcome. With no known form of income, they did require certain commodities, and one general store, not in Aidensfield but in Ashfordly, made the mistake of trusting them by supplying them with groceries on credit. The commune members took full advantage of that generosity – they never paid, although they did offer to perform some work in lieu. One of their plans was to offer to deliver groceries to the surrounding villages, but timely advice by one of our constables soon alerted the grocer to that risk. For every delivery they made, they would probably help themselves to a few items.

The great British public would find itself supporting these parasites. In addition to their known activities, they were suspected of helping themselves to the occasional bottle of milk from doorsteps, they had filled their cars' tanks with petrol at local garages and not paid their bills, they had persuaded the coal merchant to deliver a ton into their coal house and had not paid him . . . and so the problems began to multiply.

Within a year, every small business in the area found itself involuntarily supporting the commune. As one businessman said to me, 'If they'd come and asked for a basket of apples, I'd have given them one, but to pretend to buy one and then not pay – well, that's dishonest.'

His words did sum up the general attitude of the villagers. If the commune had genuinely wished to establish itself with the good will of the local people, that good will was available, but these hippies had abused it. They had resorted to cheating, and that was unforgiveable. Had they pleaded they were honest but poor, voluntary support would have been forthcoming, perhaps with a request for some kind of return assistance in and around the village.

A secondary aspect was their suspected involvement in drugs. We did receive information that some of the hippies were involved with soft drugs, cannabis being named. We heard rumours of parties at which the cannabis was smoked, these being weekend affairs when dozens of like-minded people flocked to Owlet Hall to take advantage of its remote location. Our drugs officer did raid the place from time to time, but no drugs were ever found. We never did know with any certainty whether or not drugs were being used, but the rumours persisted, and so our drugs officers continued with their raids. This did make the public uneasy, many of the local parents being concerned that their children might be tempted to try the drugs at discos or in the pubs and cafés of the district.

The combination of unsettling rumour and established facts meant that poor old William Barr found himself very unpopular. Several villagers blamed him for their problems, claiming, in their ignorance, that he should never have let the property to them. But William was helpless. There was nothing he could do to remove them; few seemed to understand that. There was nothing in criminal law to make their occupation illegal, and therefore nothing I could do to help him. The hippies knew their rights – William could never force them to leave. But they must have sensed that he was contemplating some kind of action, because they succeeded in boarding up the windows and fixing their own locks to the doors. The house was never left empty – one of them was always present.

Eventually, poor old William came to see me.

'Mr Rhea,' – he looked weary and worried – 'them hippies 'ave been in Owlet for more than a year now, and 'ave you seen t'state of it? Terrible! You'd think they'd 'ave a bit o' respect for other folks's property. My pigs never made sike a mess. Isn't there owt you can do?'

'Sorry, Bill, I can't. They know I can't, which makes it worse! Tenancy problems are not a police matter. I don't think you'd get a court order to evict them either, because if you claimed they'd damaged the place, they'd say they'd improved and repaired it, which in some ways they have. Have you got a solicitor who might advise you?'

'No, but the NFU gives advice. They said t'same as you.'

He stood behind the counter of my tiny office, and I felt sorry for him. I wished there was something someone could do, but at that time there was a gap in the law which permitted squatters to take over empty houses and live in them rent-free and to the detriment of the owners. The Labour government then in power refused to change the law, and by the 1970s this was a very common problem for property-owners. Poor old Bill was a victim of this uncaring attitude.

'Folks is blaming me,' he said. 'They owe money here, there and everywhere, they're pinching things, they've turned the house into a rubbish dump . . . now, t'locals is saying it's all my fault.'

And then, as he spoke, I remembered reading of a similar case in a village in some remote part of England. I could not remember precisely which village or even the date, but I did remember the story.

'Bill,' I said, 'I remember a similar case, a few years back. This farmer had squatters in his hand's cottage, down a lane. They took it over, just like yours.'

'And what did 'e do, Mr Rhea?'

'He put a swarm of bees through their kitchen window,' I said. 'And then, when the squatters all rushed out of the place, he put his bull in. He made the house into a home for his prize bull. That cleared 'em out,' I chuckled.

'I 'aven't got a bull,' he said seriously, then added wickedly, 'but I 'ave a useful awd tup.' A tup is the local name for a ram. And off he went, chuckling to himself. As he reached the gate, he turned and called, 'Awd Robbie Mullen owes me a favour.'

Robbie Mullen was a retired railway man who lived at Elsinby, and I knew he kept bees; I'd called upon his services from time to time when a local swarm had required attention.

I awaited developments, but nothing happened until the following May, which, I was to learn, was the time most swarms of bees occur. When a young queen bee is ready to leave the hive, half the resident workers swarm around her, and as she leaves, they cluster about her, going wherever she goes. The others remain with the resident queen. After leaving, the new queen settles on a tree or a fence to wait while several of the workers find her a new home, whereupon she joins them to establish a colony.

Awd Robbie, being an expert, waited until his bees were swarming. As luck would have it, he captured two swarms. He and Bill, with the ram in his pick-up truck, drove out to Owlet Hall early one morning and thrust the two buzzing swarms into the open windows of the house. The result was pandemonium. Eight o r ten hippies, with angry bees buzzing around their long hair, bolted nude from the house, whereupon a huge ram, seeing the open door, bolted inside.

Quite suddenly, and with a minimum of legal bantering, Owlet Hall had a different family of squatters.

Bill was on hand too and swiftly replaced the locks, later throwing from the windows the tatty belongings of his unwanted guests. I did not turn up that day, for I had no wish to delay their departure by having to deal with two untaxed cars on the road – I wanted to see no psychedelic cars at all and no long-haired alternative members of society. I just wanted rid of them.

And so they vanished, to inflict their unwelcome presence upon someone else. Bill recovered his ram, which, it seemed, had a propensity for rushing headlong into open doorways, but Robbie left his two swarms of bees in the old house. They did not stay.

'I reckon t'smell put 'em off,' he said with all seriousness.

All the belongings left behind were burned, and Bill sold the house to a builder who wanted to demolish it so that he could acquire the stone. And so, within a further year, Owlet Hall disappeared without trace.

In gratitude for my unofficial advice, Bill gave me a pot of honey which, according to Awd Robbie, was made by the very bees who did such a good job on those flower people.

8 *Grave Problems*

I love to lose myself in a mystery.
Sir Thomas Browne (1605–82)

Many police officers conclude their careers without ever having been involved in a murder investigation. I'm sure that some never cherish the desire for that experience, but because murder is constantly regarded as the worst of all crimes, there persists within many officers an ambition to arrest a murderer. If the satisfaction of making that arrest is never achieved, they wish to be a small part of the investigation; there is a certain pride at being part of a murder inquiry team, especially a successful one.

During my time as the village constable at Aidensfield, I never achieved that distinction. If murder had been committed on my patch, the mighty CID would have been called in. Many experienced detectives would have descended upon the locality to take over the investigation, and I might have been co-opted because of my local knowledge, but my role would not have been a primary one, only one of support.

Nonetheless, from time to time murders committed in distant parts did involve me. Occasionally a death in a far-off town would have links with my patch and, for example, I might have to interview the driver of a car who had driven past the scene of the killing at or about the material time.

One infamous crime which involved me on its fringes was the notorious 'Moors Murders' case. Although these crimes are forever associated with the Yorkshire moors, the moors in question are about a hundred miles to the west of those upon which I worked. They were spread across the borders of Lancashire and the West Riding of Yorkshire, while I served in the North Riding of Yorkshire. These 'Yorkshires' were two distinct counties, each with its own county police force; Lancashire was regarded as foreign territory.

The victims of Ian Brady and Myra Hindley had been buried high on those Pennine moors and there seemed little or no connection with my quiet part of Yorkshire. After the couple's conviction, however, I found myself involved in the aftermath. A man and wife whom I shall call Matt and Peggy Copeland had been watching television when a programme about the Moors Murders was shown. One of the photographs was the highly publicized full-face portrait of Myra Hindley, taken when she was looking at her most gaunt and ghastly. Upon seeing that photograph, Peggy Copeland felt sure she had seen that woman accompanied by a man; she was utterly convinced she had seen Myra Hindley digging somewhere upon the North York Moors at least a year prior to her arrest. She could not swear that the man on the moors was Ian Brady, but she never doubted she had seen Hindley.

The time had been early October, the day had been a Sunday, and the Copelands had been alone. As they had parked their car beside a lonely moorland road to enjoy a picnic, so the haunting face of a woman had appeared above a slight hillock. It was swiftly followed by a man's, and both of them stared briefly at the parked car, then vanished down the other side of the moorland mound. The man had had a spade in his hands and appeared to have been digging.

Mrs Copeland thought nothing more about this curious incident until much later, when that face of Myra Hindley had stared from her television screen. She was convinced it was the face of the woman she'd seen on the moors. She discussed her worries with her husband, and for a few days the couple lived with the awesome suspicion that they might have been parked near a murder victim's grave on the North York Moors. Uncertain what to do next, they read as much as they could about the case, to see if there were any known links with the North York Moors, but none was mentioned. Eventually they decided to visit their local police station to air their concern; this was at Peterlee in County Durham.

After exhaustive interviews, the detectives in Durham were sufficiently convinced by Peggy's story to launch an investigation. The snag was that, by this time, many months had elapsed since Peggy's sighting, and furthermore, neither she nor her husband was sufficiently knowledgeable about the North York Moors to pinpoint the precise location. They had toured the moors that Sunday without any pre-arranged plan; they did not really know their way round; neither could recall any particular village or view-point. Following a meeting about the situation, Durham CID decided that the Copelands should revisit the moors in an attempt to find both the place where they had halted for their picnic, and the mound behind which the suspicious man and woman had disappeared.

But the point of search was within Britain's largest area of open heather: there are 553 square miles inside the national park boundaries, with hundreds of miles of roads and an enormous variety of view-points. It was therefore decided that the Copelands should describe, as best they could, the route they had taken and the sights which remained in their memories. From that, an officer who was familiar with the moors would attempt, with their co-operation, to trace their picnic site.

I was selected for that job. In an unmarked police car, I had to tour the moors with the Copelands, and we had to do all within our power to locate that place. It sounded easy, but I knew it wasn't going to be. I suggested that we select a weekend which corresponded to their first visit, i.e. during early October, because the colours, the contours and even the sunlight would make conditions almost identical to that first visit. This was agreed.

At dawn one Sunday morning in October, therefore, Durham CID ferried the Copelands to Guisborough, a market town on the northern tip of the moors. I drove there to meet them.

I had been allowed to use Sergeant Blaketon's official car, immaculate in its black livery. He had checked the milometer, the tyres, the water and oil, and he had also noted there was not a scratch or patch of dirt on his vehicle.

'I want my car back in this condition, Rhea,' he reminded me as I drove off.

Armed with maps, books and photographs of the moors, I

met my companions for the day and, over a coffee in a small café, we tried to identify their route. They had enjoyed a coffee in this very café on that other visit, which made it a perfect starting-point. As a rare treat, I could pay for their coffee from official funds, because I had been issued with a small sum of money towards our subsistence for the day.

Having met this sincere couple, I was looking forward to the task. The Copelands were in their late thirties or early forties and were a genuine, down-to-earth man and woman who had found themselves in a curious situation. I did my best to assure them that they were not wasting their time or mine, for that worry seemed uppermost in their minds. I'm sure I convinced them that we considered a reconstruction of their experience meritworthy, otherwise we should not have agreed to undertake this journey.

Having thoroughly discussed our plans, we sallied forth across the splendid moors. There is no need to repeat all the details of that long and somewhat arduous trip, save to say that we covered every mile of main road within the moors and a good many leagues upon minor roads. We examined every picnic site and halting-place that I knew; we stopped, we reversed, we retraced our steps, we motored down lanes and byways and we examined mounds and bumps from every conceivable angle. We explored every possible site from every possible position. We lunched at a lovely pub and enjoyed coffees, ice-creams and soft drinks as, from time to time, we needed a break and refreshment.

As darkness fell we had not positively identified the location. We had found several 'possibles' which we marked on the Ordnance Survey map, but none proved, without doubt, to be the place where Peggy believed she had set eyes on Myra Hindley. Because darkness prevented any further exploration, I now had the task of driving my charges back to Peterlee, and it was with some sadness at our lack of success that I left the moors for that journey half-way through County Durham.

Upon arrival at the Copelands' neat little house, I was invited in; we organized some fish and chips for ourselves. I met their 15-year-old son, Paul, as we shared the table over our succulent meal. Never have fish and chips tasted so good. We discussed our trip, always trying just one more avenue in the hope we would produce an answer, but we did not. I assured them that, in my own future journeys over the moors, I would forever be alert to any possible location.

After I'd eaten, Peggy and Matt insisted I visit their son's pride and joy. I went through the back door of the house and found myself in a long, narrow extension which reeked of mice. There were hundreds of them – white mice galore, large ones, little ones, old ones and young ones, grey ones and pure white ones, mottled ones and spotty ones . . . I had never seen so many mice in one place. They were all in cages with wire fronts, all gnawing at titbits and all seeming content. Having dutifully admired them, I prepared to say my farewells and thank-yous. But as I hovered in the doorway, Peggy bade me a fond goodbye and handed me a memento of my day's duty – a small wooden cage containing two white mice! It had a glass front and two compartments, one filled with hay for sleeping upon and the other equipped with a treadmill for exercise. A tiny hole separated the two. My new friends were sniffing at me from their bedroom.

'No, really, I can't . . .' I said, thinking of Mary's reaction when I returned home.

'We'd like you to have them,' she said with the utmost sincerity. 'It's a small way of thanking you for your patience and time today. We really did enjoy the outing, even if we didn't find the place.'

I did not have the heart to refuse this gift, and so I placed my two mice on the floor of the police car, bade the Copelands farewell and set about the sixty-mile drive home. The mice squeaked from time to time but I returned to Ashfordly police station with car and mice intact. Sergeant Blaketon was waiting for me. His first task was to stalk around the car to examine it for dents, damage and dirt.

'Rhea, this car is like a midden! Look at it! Mud from fore to aft, mud as high as the roof, and mud thick enough to plant potatoes in. Where the hell have you been?'

'The moors, Sergeant, searching for evidence of a serious crime. The moorland tracks can be dirty, you know . . .'

He grumbled at length about the mud but found no damage. I followed him into the office to make my report. He listened with deep interest as I outlined every mile of my journey, with a glowing account of what we had discovered and a factual account of what we had not traced. From time to time, he quizzed me on portions of the trek which I might have omitted or forgotten, but I gained the impression he was satisfied with the outcome. He concluded the interview by saying I would have to clean the car in the morning. I assured him I would come to Ashfordly first thing – and conveniently forget to remind him that tomorrow was my day off. If he insisted I wash the car *tomorrow*, he'd have to authorize my overtime.

On this strange day, our duty had been done – we had examined the claim put forward by the Copelands, but it had proved of no value to the detectives engaged on the Moors Murder inquiry.

Before I left the office, Blaketon, in an uncharacteristic show of gratitude, said, 'Well done, Rhea. Submit a detailed written report as soon as you can. Include everything. I'll authorize overtime payment for today's duty. You've put in some long hours and I trust they were worthwhile.'

'I think so, Sergeant.'

'So, having spent an entire day with the Copelands, what do you make of them?'

'They were genuine in their belief,' I said. 'I like them, they were good people.'

'Are you saying we've some murder victims buried on our patch?' he put to me.

'No,' I said. 'I'm saying I believe Mr and Mrs Copeland were honest in their actions. I truly believe Mrs Copeland thought she had seen Myra Hindley. Whether she did is another matter; that's something I can't answer.'

'We'll send your report to Durham CID, and they'll get in touch with the murder team. You realize you might have to do the whole thing again?'

'I'll do it, if it's necessary,' I assured him, adding that it might have to wait until next year in the same season, due to the appearance of the landscape and the light.

'Good man. Well, young Rhea, let's get you home to Aidensfield. It's late.'

As he settled in the driving-seat to ferry me home, I climbed into the passenger side of his official car and lifted the mouse cage onto my lap.

'What the hell have you got there, Rhea? It pongs a good deal, I might say.'

'A pair of white mice, Sergeant,' I said inanely.

'You mean this is the result of your day's duty on a major murder investigation? You mean that you've nothing more to show for it than a pair of white mice?'

He was staring straight ahead in the darkness as he started the engine, so I could not see the expression on his face. Was he angry or was he winding me up?

'It is one outcome,' I had to stand my corner. 'A bit of light relief after a hard day. Mr and Mrs Copeland thought the children would like them.'

'I should imagine they would.' Then he chuckled. 'But what's your wife going to think? Who's going to clean them out? Who's going to feed them, Rhea? And are they male and female? If they are, my lad, you'll have millions of mice before you have time to find a cat . . .'

He went on and on about the drawbacks of keeping pet mice as he drove me back to Aidensfield.

When I arrived, the house was in darkness. Mary and the children were in bed, and all were fast asleep. I crept in, clutching the cage and its two cheerful inhabitants, and placed them on a shelf in the kitchen. I fed them supper from the mixture of grains and nuts given to me by Paul Copeland, covered the cage with a duster to keep out the draughts and crawled upstairs to bed. I was exhausted and fell into a deep sleep within seconds.

Next morning Mary awoke before me and trotted downstairs. Her loud shrieks soon aroused me.

Half asleep, I rushed down, forgetting the mice and thinking something awful had happened. I found Mary in the kitchen with the duster in her hands as she stared in astonishment at the two bright-eyed mice.

'What on earth are these?' she demanded.

'Presents,' I said. 'For the children.'

'Oh no, they're not,' she retorted. 'Just you get rid of those this very morning!'

She went on at some length, but the children had heard the commotion and came downstairs to see what was happening. All of them fell heavily and immediately in love with the mice. Amid much persuasion, Mary allowed us to keep them and soon grew fond of their presence, even if they did become a wee bit pungent at times. Happily, they were of the same sex, although I'm not sure which, so they did not reproduce. They lived on that shelf for many years, growing gracefully old, as pet mice do, while enjoying the occasional romp around the house. I did not think that naming them Ian and Myra was at all correct, neither was Matt and Peggy, and so, for reasons which escape me, we called them Ebb and Flo.

But we never undertook a further search of the North York Moors, nor did I ever learn whether the murder team had examined any of the possible sites we had identified. The mystery of Peggy Copeland's unusual sighting remains unresolved.

Another murder mystery was even more curious.

The date was 8 June when a postman hurried into Ashfordly police station; it was around 10 a.m., and by chance I was in the office.

He told me that that morning, while on his rounds, he'd been driving past a clump of pine trees on the moors behind Ashfordly when he'd noticed a small wooden cross planted in the earth. It had not been there before that day. It was adorned with ribbons, and the turf and soil beside it had been newly dug over. I asked him for a precise location and he showed me on an Ordnance Survey map. The clump of trees was beside a lonely moorland road which led through Lairsbeck to serve a few isolated farms before petering out upon the heights of the moors.

I thanked him and decided to have a look at the scene before taking any further action. I found it just as he had described. The cross stood about two feet high and had been fashioned from two hazel twigs. White ribbons dangled from the arms, and it stood within a circle of some two dozen pine trees, with not a cottage or farm in sight. The cross was firmly upright in a thick grassy patch, and immediately in front of it was a small area of recently dug earth. My own guess was that the earth was very fresh – it might even have been dug over that morning; certainly it was not more than a day or two old. It was the size of a human grave, not one small enough for a cat or a dog. Remaining at the site, I radioed the control room at Eltering and outlined the situation. Sergeant Bairstow said he would liaise with me at the scene, his estimated time of arrival being half an hour. I was instructed to wait and not touch anything.

When Charlie Bairstow arrived, he stood and looked for a long time at that odd sight, occasionally scratching his head while walking in a circle around the trees.

'What do you make of it, Nick?' he asked.

'No idea,' I said. 'Could it be a horse, a pony perhaps? A pet cow or calf? Goat? It looks as though something's been buried and commemorated, doesn't it?'

'But would anybody commemorate an animal with a cross?' he asked.

'It wouldn't surprise me,' I said, recalling that some Americans arranged weddings for dogs and birthday parties for cats. 'But who'd bury a person here and then mark the grave like that?'

'There's only one way to find out. We'll have to call in the cavalry.'

By that, he meant he'd call in the CID and their experts, for they would surely examine the grave by digging it up.

From his car radio, he summoned divisional headquarters, whereupon Detective Sergeant Gerry Connolly said he would come immediately; we had to wait yet again and not touch anything. He arrived within three-quarters of an hour and examined the lonely site.

'We'll have to dig it up,' he pronounced. 'I'll get my lads to do it – I'll need a photographer standing by. I'll radio them now while we tape off the area.'

'Anything I can do?' I asked.

'Yes, Nick, get the yellow tape from my car boot. Circle those trees with it and watch where you put your feet. If you find anything there – anything at all, leave it where it is, then tell me.'

Thus the formalities began. One or two cars passed as we worked, but at this stage we did not ask any questions, nor did we interview the few householders whose cottages occupied these remote moors. The nearest was almost half a mile away. Detective Constables Ian Shackleton and Paul Wharton arrived with spades, picks and wheelbarrow, and Detective Sergeant Marks, the photographer, arrived to record progress. The scene was now one of activity and interest, with no fewer than five police cars, lots of police officers and yellow tape, all laced with a high degree of anticipated drama.

Ian Shackleton lost no time in commencing his dig. As the earth was soft, he found it a comparatively easy task, and very soon he had a broad and deep hole. But apart from the soil and a few surprised worms, there was nothing buried there. Joined by Paul Wharton and his pick-axe, they expanded the area of digging until they covered an area of about twelve feet by six in rough terms. Having stretched beyond the boundaries of the original grave without finding anything, they dug several shallow trenches without encountering anything remotely suspicious, and then concentrated upon digging deeper into the original grave and also below the cross. Soon they came to the sub-soil, which was undisturbed. It wasn't long before we had a hole large enough to contain a small swimming-pool, and nothing to show for it but a huge pile of earth. The forlorn little wooden cross lay on one side.

'Nothing,' said Connolly eventually. 'Sod all, in fact. Nowt. Nil.'

'Does it suggest the ground's been prepared for a grave?' suggested Ian Shackleton.

'Well, we're not going to fill it in! If somebody else cares to bury summat here, let 'em!' laughed Connolly. 'Leave the earth as it is, but replace the cross. Charlie,' he addressed Sergeant Bairstow, 'get your lads to visit this place regularly, will you? Summat's being going on, but I've no idea what. See what you can turn up.'

'It's a good task for young Rhea,' beamed Sergeant Bairstow. 'How about it, Nick? See if you can find out just what's been happening here.'

'I'll do my best,' I promised.

And so we dispersed, leaving the earth around the edge of the massive hole, and the cross in its original position, albeit now in bare, upturned earth. I decided to do my best to find answers to the puzzles. Who had place the cross there and why? And who had turned over this earth, and why?

When the others had gone, I drove to the nearest cottage. It was occupied by a farm labourer and his wife who were having their afternoon tea break when I arrived. I was invited in, offered a seat at their kitchen table and given a mug of tea with a piece of fruitcake. I learned that the couple, in their fifties, were Mr and Mrs Byworth, George and Ada. I explained our actions, and George smiled. 'Aye, Mr Rhea, Ah spotted yon police cars and reckoned they'd be digging.'

'You know what's been happening there?'

'A murder, Mr Rhea. Yon trees are called Grave Wood, there's a circle of 'em. They were planted around a grave.'

'When was this?' I interrupted him.

'1895,' he said. 'My dad told me all about it. He lived here before me. It was a farmhand called John Appleton. He killed his wife and little lass and buried 'em right where you were digging. Nasty case, it was. He had no other woman, nowt like that, but he was a bit daft, only in his twenties, and he led his wife and bairn out to look at that grave. He'd dug it ready, and as they stood looking into it, wondering what it was, he killed 'em both, shot 'em. They fell into that grave and he buried 'em. He was found out, mind, and they hanged him.'

'What happened to the bodies? Do you know?'

'Aye,' he said. 'The woman and her bairn were reburied in Ashfordly churchyard. It was a funny do. They had a funny vicar then: 'e wouldn't allow the bodies to come in through t'lychgate for some reason. They had to pass t'coffins over t'church wall. T'graves are still there.'

'And somebody planted those pines in memory of them?'

'They 'ad no relations hereabouts; they came from away when Appleton got work here as a farmhand. I know because he worked on t'same farm as my dad. But they found no relations for the lass and her bairn. Nobody. So the local folks planted them trees, Mr Rhea. In memory.'

Then another aspect occurred to me.

'When was the murder in 1895?' I asked.

'8 June,' he said. '8 June 1895.'

'That's seventy years ago today,' I whispered. 'Today is 8 June.'

'Aye,' he said.

'So the digging out there? The digging before we came, and that cross? What do you know about that, Mr Byworth?'

'Nowt,' he said. 'But awd Horace Baines might know.'

'Horace Baines?' I didn't know the man.

'Used to be our roadman, retired a few years back. He lives in Ashfordly, not far from t'front gate of t'castle.'

'So why should he know?'

'He was up here at six this morning,' smiled George.

'Out for a long walk, was he?'

'No, he was digging, in Grave Wood,' he smiled almost wickedly.

I realized that if we'd asked a few questions before commencing our own digging operation, we might have saved ourselves a lot of work. But I decided the exercise had been good for those CID lads!

'So why would he be digging there?' I asked.

'You'd better ask him, Mr Rhea, cos I don't know.'

'And you don't know who put that little cross there?'

'No idea,' he said, and his wife concurred.

I thanked them for their wonderful co-operation and drove back into Ashfordly, where I had no trouble locating Horace Baines. He was in his pretty stone cottage, a truly picturesque place with honeysuckle over the front door and roses climbing over an outhouse. He led me into his garden, where I admired his flowers and vegetables.

'I'm not in trouble, am I?' he asked.

'No,' I assured him. 'It's curiosity, that's all,' and I explained my purpose.

'You'll know about the murder then?' he put to me.

'I do now,' I said. 'But I didn't know until today.'

'Well, after that lass and her bairn were killed, somebody erected a memorial stone. It stood for years, until the Second World War. Then these moors were used as tank training grounds.'

'Was this before the pines were planted?'

'Aye,' he said briefly. 'Well, I was the roadman; that length was my responsibility. I used to see that little stone every time I came this way. But when the tanks started to train here, they drove straight over it. It got pressed into the earth, Mr Rhea, and in time it got lost, overgrown mebbe.'

'I see.' I could guess what he was going to tell me.

'Well, I kept thinking I would rescue it, but you know how it was, tanks and soldiers everywhere. I never did get it rescued, so this morning, because I woke early, I thought I'd have a look for it and erect it somewhere proper. After the war, when the tanks had gone, somebody planted those trees where the grave was, so I dug in there. But I never found it. Mebbe it is still there, or mebbe somebody else has got it.'

'Our lads dug it over pretty well this morning,' I assured him. 'We dug much more than you, but we never found even a fragment.'

'It'll be somewhere about.' He sounded confident. 'Mebbe it's in a farm shed somewhere, or being used as a paving stone in a footpath or in somebody's rockery . . .'

'Is there a special reason for wanting to recover it?' I asked.

'It was my dad helped the police catch Appleton,' he said. 'He came past one day and saw Appleton digging there. When the lass and kiddie disappeared, he told the police what he'd seen – and they found the bodies. Dad would have wanted me to find that stone, you see.'

'And why did you make the effort today?' I asked him. 'You know it's seventy years today since the murder?'

'Is it? No, I hadn't realized that. I just decided to go all of a sudden. I'd been thinking about it for a week or two. Fancy me picking today of all days!'

'Thanks, it is a strange coincidence, but you have solved one mystery,' I said. 'Now, the little cross of hazel twigs. Did you put that there?'

'No,' he said. 'That wasn't me.'

'Was it there when you were digging?'

'Aye,' he said. 'It was. I moved it while I dug, but I never put it there.'

'Any idea who might have?' I pressed him. 'I'm curious, that's all. There's no official police inquiry about all this, not after all this time!'

'No idea,' he smiled. 'But you might find Mrs Gowland who lives beside the butcher's can help.'

And so I continued my enquiries by calling on Mrs Gladys Gowland, a lady of almost eighty. The uniform helped me to gain her confidence, for she was shy and cautious, but when I explained my interest, she smiled and invited me to sit down. She produced a cup of tea and a scone, then a large wooden box full of newspaper cuttings and faded photographs.

'I don't want any of this published or copied,' she said guardedly. 'I have built my collection of news cuttings about Ashfordly for many, many years, and it is my personal collection, you see.'

I had to convince her that I had no intention of removing any of her documents or of copying anything. She showed me yellowed cuttings about the murder, the trial and the funeral of the victims, a fascinating piece of local history. But apart from a lot of local colour and somewhat exaggerated drama, the cuttings did not tell me much more than Horace Baines had revealed. They shed no light at all on the mysterious little wooden cross, although a later cutting did say that the local people had planted the trees after the Second World War because the grave had been obliterated by the actions of the tanks in training.

I asked her outright: 'Mrs Gowland, when we arrived today, there was a little wooden cross near the grave. Did you put it there?'

'No,' she said, and I believed her, for how could she have trekked in secret to that location?

And so the mystery remained, and it remains to this day. I have no idea who placed that cross on the grave to two murder victims who died during the last century, without relations but with some enduring friends.

However, I did later learn that a cross was traditionally placed at the scene of a murder to prevent the ghost of the victim returning to haunt the area. That cross had to be renewed upon each anniversary of the death. In days gone by, some policemen would scratch a cross in the dust or earth near a murder victim, or sometimes it would be marked on a post or door. So was this the reason for that little wooden cross? Had it been placed there every year since the crime in order to keep at bay the ghosts of the victims? It is a fascinating thought. *It became even more fascinating when the cross reappeared on 8 June 1989*!

As a last act in this piece of unofficial research, I decided to seek the graves in Ashfordly churchyard. I ignored the modern stones as I sought an old tombstone, possibly bearing two names. It took me a long time, but I did find it.

The tombstone bore the name of Anne Appleton and her daughter Marie, who had died tragically on 8 June 1895.

The grave also bore a vase of freshly cut flowers.

9 *The Goldfish and the Goat*

Accidents will occur in the best regulated families.
Charles Dickens (1812–70)

Traffic accidents have always occupied a lot of police time and effort. As the volume and diversity of traffic have increased, so the range and number of accidents have multiplied. In the good old days before the Second World War, a serious traffic accident was unusual. Today it is common-place and can involve anything from a road roller to a bicycle, by way of articulated lorry, mobile crane, tank, car or caravan. I have included some tales of accidents in previous *Constable* volumes.

Because traffic accidents are so frequent, police officers tend to regard them as routine, but for the unfortunate victims they are anything but routine. They are hurtful, traumatic, expensive, time-wasting, annoying, upsetting and horrible. In many cases, I'm sure that a driver suffers only one serious accident in his or her lifetime, or maybe none at all. Not every minor bump is recorded, but an accident at which the police officiate is something of a rarity for most drivers.

One such driver was 70-year-old Alf Partridge. I had known him for years, for he had been a friend of my family for as long as I could remember, and he was a wonderful character. Rather short in height, he was plump and balding, with a ready smile and an easy manner which charmed everyone. No one had a bad word to say about Alf: he was everyone's friend. He ran a small garage-cum-filling-station in a moorland village called Milthorpe, which was not within my own area of patrol, although from time to time he did cross the moors into my patch. In those cases, he was generally performing a taxi run, his taxi being one part of his village business.

He was also a peat-cutter, for he owned rights to one of the moorland peat bogs from which he supplied a small range of customers. For this, he would drive onto the moors in the spring with his special peat-cutting tools to cut a portion from the bog. After a 'dess' was cut and the face was 'sliped' to deter the rain, the peat sods were stacked or 'rickled' on the 'ligging' or lying ground. Here it was left to dry in the moorland breezes before delivery or use. Special hicking (hand) barrows were used for transporting the peat at the site. The entire operation was fascinating to observe. I don't think Alf undertook his peat-cutting for any real commercial reason – he found it a relaxing change from his garage and taxi business, although he did burn peat in his delightful cottage.

But the things I most vividly remember were the scrupulously tidy and completely efficient cars which he used. They were immaculate inside and out, their engines ticked over like silken watches, and every part was meticulously maintained and cared for.

From time to time when we were children, we would be taxied to various places because our parents did not own a car, and indeed, when I joined the police service at the age of sixteen, I was driven to my interview at force headquarters by Alf in one of his magnificent taxis. Although the car was not pretentious in any way, I can still recall its sheer magic, its smooth drive, its aura of total reliability and efficiency.

Everything about Alf was clean and pleasant; even his garage premises were tidy and neat, for he had trained his men to respect his own high standards. It was like walking into an exhibition rather than a working country garage. Every tool not in use was returned to its allocated space; every piece of scrap metal or other waste was collected and removed, every mess was cleared up and the floor kept clean. Even the window, which overlooked the street, was a joy. It displayed spares, such as tyres, plugs and wash leathers, and he took the trouble to decorate them seasonally with Christmas crackers, Easter eggs or whatever was topical. And no one ever saw Alf lose his temper or become flustered – his whole existence was so well planned that his passage through life was calm, smooth and trouble-free.

It was a matter of pride for Alf that he had never been involved in a traffic accident. In all his years of motoring, he had never once had a scrape with another vehicle, nor even a scratch from nature's defences. The bodies of his cars were immaculate, not even the thorns of the hedgerows or the horns of moorland sheep daring to mark his polished paintwork and glistening chrome.

But one sunny morning in April, on one of the moorland's most remote highways, Alf felt that his reputation had been shattered. His legendary calm was decidedly ruffled, because he was involved in an accident, or perhaps it was a near-miss?

He was driving his black, shining and immaculate Humber Snipe towards his peat bog; he towed a trailer he had built, and it contained his specially angled peat spade, a gripe, his hicking barrow and assorted tools. It was a fine, dry morning and the roads were empty. Indeed, the rough roads across these heights were nearly always empty, their only traffic being the local moorland farmers and peat-cutters who came this way from time to time. Not many outsiders found their way over these heights then, although that situation has now changed. Today that narrow moorland road is surfaced and, because it is shown on tourist maps, it now suffers regular passage of traffic. Alf, had he been alive today, would have been horrified.

But on that spring morning in the mid-1960s Alf had no thoughts of meeting other vehicles. He had traversed these moors for years without seeing another motor along his route. The regular passage of horse-drawn vehicles and coaches had ended, and major, well-surfaced roads had been built through the dales. They coped with visitors, buses and routine traffic.

And so year after year Alf had driven to his peat bog at dawn to cut the required number of sods, and year after year he had driven home contented and happy with his unpressurized life. There were no cars, no traffic lights, no roundabouts, no signposts, no bollards and no houses – there was nothing but a rough track for use by the likes of Alf Partridge.

But one morning another car dared to use the primitive road. At one point the track dips down a gentle slope where it crosses a moorland beck before rising at the other side. Midway down the first slope, in the direction in which Alf was driving that morning, a minor track enters the highway from the right. It was originally a drovers' road and, as cars were becoming more numerous, some daring drivers occasionally made use of it to cross the moors from the northernmost parts of Eskdale. It was proving to be a useful short-cut. At its junction with Alf's road, however, it was not readily visible. It emerged from between high banks of heather; indeed, a stranger would not even realize there was a junction until arriving, for there was no road sign to announce the fact.

As Alf had chugged along his regular route, so a young man in a bright yellow Austin Healey Sprite sports car was hurtling along the drovers' road. In his low-slung car, he was concealed by the high banks of heather and did not see Alf, and Alf did not see him. As Alf approached the junction, so the yellow flash bolted across his route, apparently from nowhere. From his right, it passed directly into Alf's path.

Alf reacted with remarkable speed. He swung his steering wheel savagely to the left, as a result of which he found himself bouncing across the open moorland with his trailer of tools clanking behind. The incident so unnerved him that, for the briefest of moments, he forgot to brake, and so his lovely car cruised for some distance across the smooth grassy patch between the heather patches, then came to an ignominious halt in a bog of sphagnum moss. The engine stalled.

It pitched Alf forward, and within a very few moments the car began to sink. Alf was still inside, but not injured. He was able to observe the yellow sports car disappearing up the slope opposite but had not the time to take its registration number. He was alone to his fate as his car sank slowly into the mire, and so he decided to abandon his precious vehicle. Happily, the bog was not too deep, so when Alf stepped out, he found himself on a firm base, albeit up to the thighs in peat-coloured water and thick yellow mud as his precious Humber sank at his side. It halted when the mire was half-way up its doors.

The problem was what to do next.

Unknown to Alf, the young man in the yellow sports car had halted in Rannockdale to ring the police. Without giving his name, he said he'd seen a car run off the road at Bluestone Beck. The call was received at Eltering police station, and a map revealed that the location was literally yards inside our patch.

I was in Sergeant Blaketon's car at the time. With him acting as driver, we were undertaking an early morning inspection of quarries which had explosives stores and were using the occasion to check the accuracy of our Explosives Register. Then we were diverted to Bluestone Beck.

As we drove down the slope towards Alf's bogged-down car, I recognized him. I said, 'Good Lord, it's Alf!'

'Do you know the driver, Rhea?' asked Sergeant Blaketon.

'Yes, he's been a family friend for years,' I said, and then explained my childhood knowledge of Alf, reinforcing the fact that he had never had an accident or suffered damage to his precious cars.

'In that case, Rhea,' Sergeant Blaketon said formally, 'I had better deal with this accident. If there is a question of prosecuting him for careless driving or something more serious, we can't have a family friend involved in the legal processes.'

'I'd do a fair job on the report, Sergeant.'

'I will deal with it, Rhea,' he said with an air of finality.

As we halted near the scene, I could see Alf furiously digging with his peat-cutting spade. He was throwing masses of muck around as he tried to find some solid ground for his rear wheels – in this mess, they only spun uselessly as he tried to force his car out of the bog. And he was in a terrible state. He was smothered in grime; his clothes, hair and face were dripping with wet sphagnum moss.

It was evident that he did not recognize me when our police car halted a few yards away. In his present highly charged condition, he might not have recognized his own mother, but he had not seen me for years and had no idea I was concealed within that uniform. Sergeant Blaketon strode across the sound piece of moorland to speak to him, as I waited with the car. And I must admit I was amazed at Alf's angry and belligerent response.

'There's no need for you buggers to come here snooping,' were his first words. 'I can get myself out of this . . . I don't need you lot laughing at me . . .'

'We received a report of an accident . . .' began Oscar Blaketon.

'Accident? What accident? There's been no accident. I haven't hit anybody. There's been no crash. No injuries. I was forced off the road, that's what. If I hadn't run down here, I'd have hit him . . . I avoided an accident . . . the silly bugger . . . look at this . . . what a bloody mess . . . I want none of this in the bloody papers and you can keep me out of court if that's what's in your mind . . . so how am I going to get out of here, eh? Just you answer me that!'

'There has been an accident,' chanted Blaketon, adopting a rather formal attitude. 'If, owing to the presence of a motor vehicle on a road, an accident occurs whereby damage is caused to a motor vehicle other than that vehicle, then so far as the law is concerned, it is an accident.

'It conforms to the definition in the Road Traffic Act,' Blaketon went on. 'If another car's driver forced you off the road, then he caused the accident – and the fact that you are sitting up to your eyebrows in plother means there has been an accident, an untoward incident, an unwanted event.'

'Then get after that yellow car and book him for not stopping, Sergeant,' bellowed Alf. 'And what about towing me out of here?'

'You'll need a breakdown truck for that.'

'Well, I can't do much about getting one from here, can I? Can't you blokes radio somebody? Get my mate, Eddie Brookes, Milthorpe 253. He'll come for me. And what about that other idiot, eh? Why aren't you chasing him and his yellow peril? Running folks off the road like this . . .'

'Is there any damage?' shouted Blaketon.

'How should I know?' snapped Alf. 'Look at it! How can I say what harm's done under all this muck? God knows what my underside's hit under this moss . . . I could have knocked the sump off, broken an axle, but I'm stuck solid, I am . . .'

As Alf chuntered and cursed, Blaketon came across to me and sat in the car. He was in a surprisingly gentle mood, and I must admit I was not accustomed to seeing him like this.

'Rhea,' he said, 'you know this character. He sounds a bit irate to me. Now, the way I see it is that there might be a dangerous driving case against the chap in the sports car, if we can find him.'

'And if we can prove it,' I chipped in. 'It's Alf's word against his; Alf might have been half asleep. I know he's an old friend of my parents, but, well, he is getting on a bit.'

'True, very true. But if this Alf's car is not damaged, it is doubtful if there is a reportable accident, eh? In other words, we are not wanted here. We are not duty-bound to deal with this, unless he complains about the other driver.'

'I'd like to get him out of his mess,' I said.

'Then radio them at Eltering and ask them to call his friend, Rhea.'

As Blaketon sat at my side, oddly reluctant to exercise his awesome authority over poor old Alf, I did this small favour. Our Eltering office contacted Eddie Brookes with the story, and he said he'd come immediately with his breakdown truck to tow Alf from the bog.

'I think, under the circumstances, we should depart, Rhea,' said Blaketon. 'I agree this is one driver's word against another, and if this man is a friend of yours, he might talk himself into a careless driving charge if I quiz him too much. You must admit he's a bit irate, he's not thinking straight, he might say too much and drop himself further into the mire.' And he glanced at the bog as he chuckled at his own joke.

'He has good reason,' I said.

'He had no reason to talk to me like that,' said Blaketon. 'I'm only doing my duty. I'm not responsible for his accident.'

'Sergeant,' I said, 'this is his first accident in more than fifty years of driving. I'm not surprised he's a bit angry, especially as it's not his fault. I'm sure you would be the same. I know you have a clean driving record . . .'

'Then let's leave him,' he said quickly. 'If I stay until the breakdown truck arrives, Rhea, I might see the damage on his car, and I might make it an official traffic accident, which means he could be the subject of a report for alleged careless driving.'

'Thanks, Sergeant,' I said. 'Can I have a word with him before we leave?'

'Right ho,' he said, not offering to accompany me. This was not the normal Blaketon, I realized, and I could not understand why he was so gentle with Alf.

I wandered over to Alf, who, upon seeing my approach, launched into a tirade of abuse against everyone, especially drivers of yellow sports cars. But when I removed my cap, he recognized me.

'God! It's young Nick!'

'Hello, Mr Partridge.' I used the name I'd called him in my youth. 'You've got yourself into a bit of pickle, eh?'

That set him off again, but I calmed him down by saying we were leaving, and explained the reasons, adding that Eddie's truck was on his way.

'This'll ruin my record, Nick,' said poor old Alf. 'All these years without a scratch and now this . . .'

'It won't ruin it,' I said. 'There'll be no official entry in our files, especially if you don't make a formal complaint about that yellow car.'

'But my car'll be ruined. Look at it, up to the doorposts in muck and plother . . .'

But we left it at that. He decided not to prosecute the yellow peril. If he had made a formal complaint, it would have been difficult, if not impossible, to prove the case, and Alf would have been called as a witness. That alone would have destroyed his own long record. I felt we had achieved a diplomatic result.

As I drove Blaketon back to the office, I suddenly realized why he had been such a wonderful help to poor old Alf. A few months earlier, during the snowfalls of that winter, there'd been a rumour about Sergeant Blaketon's driving into a ploughed field somewhere in these dales. He'd been off duty at the time, but it had required a farmer and his tractor to drag him out; no official report had been made and there'd been no damage to his car. We had heard through gossip, but Blaketon himself had never said a word about it. I wondered if Alf or Eddie had been involved in that. Obviously Alf didn't remember it, but it did help me to understand why Blaketon was sympathetic to poor old Alf's predicament.

Several months later I saw Alf in Eltering. He was driving the same car, and it looked immaculate.

'Hello, Mr Partridge,' I greeted him, then added, 'The car looks great!'

'There wasn't a mark on it,' he said. 'It was mucky and wet, but there wasn't a scratch. That sphagnum made a soft landing for it.'

'So your record's clean, eh?'

'Aye,' he said. 'Thanks to that sergeant of yours.'

Another harrowing tale involved a serious accident to a caravan unit. A couple from Norfolk, where real hills are a rarity, came to the North York Moors for a caravanning holiday. They decided to tour an area where there are numerous hills of 1-in-3 gradient (33 per cent) and where anything up to a gradient 1-in-10 (10 per cent) rarely warrants a 'Steep Hill' warning notice. For the local people, these gradients present no problem; for the tourist, they can be terrifying, and most certainly they do sift the good drivers from the bad or hopeless.

We call these hills 'banks'. There is the White Horse Bank near Kilburn whose gradient was not, in my time at Aidensfield, mentioned, in case no one believed it. There's the fascinating, winding Chimney Bank at Rosedale, which even the locals admit is 'brant'. That means 'steep' in the dialect of the region, i.e. about 1-in-3 (33 per cent). There are many others, especially in Eskdale, but one which causes a certain amount of angst among dithering drivers is Sutton Bank near Thirsk. It is not particularly steep, but it is a mile long with three gradients, the first being 1-in-4, the second 1-in-5 and the final one 1-in-4.

Until recently, tourists would examine their maps to see that this A-class road led to Scarborough from the Al and would head towards it. Even if the tourist maps do include a 'Steep Hill' symbol at these locations, few of these dreamy visitors realize what it means, and so, during a typical English summer, these banks are often blocked by motorists for whom the normal occasions for selection of first gear are as common as their birth or funeral. In the case of Sutton Bank, it was frequently blocked by little men in Morris Minors who tried to tow caravans to the summit. The failure rate was high, even when the towing car was a powerful one such as a Volvo or a Mercedes, and a local farmer with a powerful tractor made a fortune from towing such incompetents to safety on the plateau above. Happily, caravans are now banned from this hill – but the hills are not to blame; it is the drivers who are the problem. The local people have no trouble with the hill – even our ancient lady drivers can cope.

Unfortunately for Mr John Plumpton, he was one of those hapless drivers. Utterly hopeless, he braked on every corner, even on level roads; he could not reverse into a parking space and had never previously towed a caravan. His wife, Sally, wasn't much help either, because she couldn't drive at all and was nervous at anything faster than 25 mph. For a man of his calibre to venture into our hilly moors and dales with a heavy load forever on his tail was an act of sheer stupidity. It is like climbing Everest in plimsolls.

It is times like these when police officers ponder upon their role in society, for so often we spend time clearing up the mess left by the nation's hopeless and incompetents. In this case, John Plumpton's lack of skill almost had fatal consequences.

For reasons which are not clear, he decided to take his caravan down Sorrel Bank, which descends from the moors into Maddleskirk. Almost a mile long, it is a narrow, twisting bank with gradients of around 1-in-4 (25 per cent), which is not particularly steep for this area. At the foot, the bank emerges onto a well-used road which leads into the village via the floor of the dale. The latter is not a classified road, so at that time there were no junction markings, and in fact there was no 'Steep Hill' sign on Sorrel Bank. The road is very narrow, being only the width of one vehicle, and the approach along the top skirts a pine forest as it affords superb views across the Vale of York. When it reaches Sorrel Brow Farm, the road suddenly dips as it begins its rapid descent towards the western end of Maddleskirk.

John and Sally Plumpton sailed majestically into this dip, and before John realized what was happening, his unit was gathering speed. Very quickly, the combined weight of car and caravan urged the wheels to turn at an ever-increasing pace. With no places to run off the road, it was like descending one of those fairground chutes, each corner bending so sharply and dropping ever downwards that the road beyond was out of sight. I don't think John actually steered his car down that hill. I think the camber of the road and the high verges guided the front wheels along the road surface without any effort by him. In fact, I don't think John had any control at all; when I interviewed him some time later, he could not remember even having changed to a lower gear.

In simple terms, he panicked. As the car and its caravan bolted down Sorrel Bank, he simply let it run free, and it knew where to go. In his panic, he either missed his brake pedal or omitted to use it; he utterly failed to make use of his gears for additional control, and it was a classic case of driving at its very worst. Men of this calibre ought to be severely tested every few years – they are a liability to themselves and to others. The outcome of Plumpton's panic was that this huge moving combination of run-away vehicles careered down that long, winding hill totally out of control. By the grace of God, nothing was travelling the other way. The road was empty at the time. Fortunately the road which formed the junction at the bottom was also empty, and so the car and caravan hurtled across but came to an ignominious end at that point.

Opposite the exit from Sorrel Bank, the verge was high but wide, and there was a hedge containing a solid sycamore tree, behind which lay a field. That field also sloped steeply from the hedge and levelled out some yards below, at which point it produced a thick clump of hawthorn trees.

John and Sally must have had a good view of this field as it rose to meet them, but as their car just missed the sycamore, the leading edge of the caravan hit it. This demolished the caravan; it disintegrated into a pile of matchwood as the car separated from it and continued down the field, rolling over several times until it came to rest among the hawthorns. The roof was flattened, the car was wrecked and the caravan lay in exploded pieces around the sycamore.

A villager called the police and ambulance, and I arrived to find this mayhem. Of the caravan, very little remained, and the family's belongings were scattered across the verge and the field, with several pairs of Sally's knickers decorating the hedge, and John's clean socks dangling from some elderberry trees. The couple were trapped in their upturned car, and we had to cut them free, both badly injured.

As I helped Sally into the ambulance, she whispered to me, 'Did you find Oliver?'

'Oliver?' I was horrified. 'No, was he in the car?'

'No,' she said weakly. 'In thc caravan.'

My heart sank. 'How old is he?'

'Four,' she said. 'It was his birthday last week. He always travels in the caravan . . .' and she drifted into unconsciousness.

As the ambulance surged away to York Hospital with its casualties, I rushed back to the debris and started my search. Oliver must have been in one of the bunks. He could be trapped anywhere.

Aided by the fire brigade who had come to cut free the Plumptons, we sifted through the wreckage but found no sign of the child. I knew that in some freak accidents children can be flung far from the wreckage, and so we arranged a full-scale search of all the shrubbery, with a more stringent examination of the wrecked car. But there was no sign of Oliver. It took us hours to examine every likely place, but the result was nil.

I radioed my office at Eltering. I explained our problem to PC John Rogers and asked if he would ring the hospital. I wanted a doctor to speak to Mrs Plumpton as soon as she regained consciousness, in an attempt to establish just where Oliver would have been lying or sitting or, indeed, whether she was mistaken. Maybe she had not brought him on this holiday? Maybe the stress of the accident had caused her to believe he was there when in fact he was with relatives? Maybe the husband could throw some light on the matter? I told John that I would remain at the scene, continuing the search, until I heard from them. I would carry out a further search of the wreckage and surrounding vegetation, even to the extent of checking every inch of the route down the bank. Maybe Oliver had been been thrown out during that nightmare descent?

With that thought dominating my mind and aided by the dedicated firemen, I climbed the hill and meticulously checked the verges and hedges, hoping against hope that I would find the boy. I did not.

Dejected, we returned to the wreckage. As I wandered among it, I noticed a movement in a man's shoe which was lying among the miasma. I stooped and found a goldfish; it was still alive. It was flicking its tail and gasping as I lifted the shoe to show the nearest fireman.

'I've some water on board!' he laughed. 'Here, there's a plastic bucket over there!'

And so we filled the bucket with water from the fire tender and plonked in the fish. With a flick of its tail, it began to swim around as if nothing had happened.

'I knew a goldfish that had been buried as dead,' said the fireman. 'Then hours later it poked its head out of the soil. It lived another three years . . .'

As we hunted yet again among the larger items, the radio called me. It was John Rogers.

'We've had words with the hospital, Nick. A doctor has spoken to Mrs Plumpton.'

'Yes?' I wanted to get this matter settled.

'Oliver was definitely in the caravan,' he said. 'We've checked and double-checked with her. She'd adamant about it. He is four, as she said, but . . .' – and he burst into laughter.

'What's the matter?' I asked.

'He's not a child, Nick.'

'Not the dog!' I groaned.

'No, he's a goldfish. Apparently he leads an adventurous life. He always goes caravanning with them; he loves travelling. Last year he jumped out of his bowl and spent the night on the floor but survived. On another occasion he got tipped down the sink by mistake but was found alive. He's a kind of James Bond among goldfish!'

I laughed quietly to myself, then said, 'Then he's done it again. This time I've found him alive and well and living in a shoe. Perhaps you'd inform Mrs Plumpton?'

'You're not serious, Nick?'

'I am. He's swimming in a plastic bucket of fire brigade water right now,' I laughed. 'He was found in a shoe, still alive. He's a lucky soul,' I added. John groaned at my awful pun. 'How are the Plumptons?' I asked.

'They'll survive,' he said. 'They've each got a few broken bones – arms and legs mainly – and lots of bruises, but they'll recover. It'll cheer them up to know that Oliver has survived, but John Plumpton says he'll never drive again.'

'Then some good's come out of this,' I thought, and added, 'I'll visit them soon. I'll need a statement from each of them in due course. And I'll take Oliver with me. He can visit them in hospital.'

'He makes a nice twist to the story,' he said, and at that awful pun I groaned as I turned away to begin the task of clearing up the mess.

I had further trouble with another animal which survived a traffic accident. In this case, a small and very decrepit van was travelling down the main street of Crampton when its steering failed. Fortunately it was not moving very rapidly at the time, a feat it was truly incapable of performing in safety, and so the resultant damage should have been negligible. It wove along the highway as its driver did his best to stop, but the brakes weren't very good either. In those few moments, it wobbled onto the footpath, glanced off a telegraph pole, mounted a low wall and overturned.

By that stage, it had arrived in the gravel driveway of a rather nice house and thus lay on its side while the driver scrambled from the passenger seat. To escape from his small van, he had to climb upwards and then leap from the chassis onto the drive. Other than its almost totally blocking the drive, there was no harm to the house or the garden – yet.

Unfortunately the rear of the van contained a very bad-tempered billy goat, and as the vehicle had overturned, so the rear doors had burst open. The goat had therefore taken the opportunity of leaving its transport, and as the driver walked shakily to the rear of the van to check things, so the goat had strolled towards the front, out of sight of the driver, the bulk of the stricken van separating them. And so, as the driver, whose name was Tony Harris, found himself standing on the footpath outside the gate of the house and staring into his empty van, his goat found itself standing in the garden.

As the goat reached the front of the overturned van, the householder, a Mr Douglas Lynton-Cross, opened his front door to see what had arrived in his garden. The goat, we were to learn in due course, was like Awd Billy Barr's ram – it had a propensity for charging through open doors. As there was no one else around against whom to direct its anger, the upset billy noticed Mr Lynton-Cross in the doorway and was thus presented with two objects of interest – and promptly lowered it head, aimed its horns and charged.

Mr Lynton-Cross, an aged man who found sudden agility, bolted into the house but, in his anxiety to reach safety, left the door partly open. The heavy and hairy goat hurtled indoors in hot pursuit and found itself in the front hall of this splendid house. At this early stage, Tony Harris had no idea where his animal had gone. As he hurried off down the High street to (a) summon help and (b) find his goat, the animal in question was exploring the ground floor of Mr Lynton-Cross's home, while its worried occupant watched from the comparative safety of the landing above. The goat wandered into the front lounge, which was where Mr Lynton-Cross kept his collection of lead soldiers. They were arrayed in their colourful uniforms in regimental order and occupied several glass display cases around the walls and indeed in the centre of the spacious room.

It seems that the goat saw another goat there; this was because some of Mr Lynton-Cross's cabinets had mirrors at the back. The purpose of the mirrors was to provide more light for the displays and to create an aura of spaciousness. But billy goats are not *au fait* with such sophisticated display techniques. The visiting beast saw its adversary and charged it. The first charge smashed that display cabinet into small pieces, bringing down the shelves and scattering soldiers across the floor as the goat sought its foe. Here and there in that room, it spotted its likeness, sometimes here, sometimes there, but always peering at it from behind show cases. It charged again and again in its attempts to defeat the threatening enemy. The devastation, accompanied by the sound of much breaking glass, must have been heart-breaking for Mr Lynton-Cross.

When the angry animal had chased the intruder from that room, it decided to seek elsewhere. It knew there was a goat in the house and hadn't yet dealt with it.

It was at that moment that Mrs Lynton-Cross, upon hearing the awful din at the front of the house, emerged from the kitchen to see what was happening. The goat was thus presented with another open door. It charged at Mrs Lynton-Cross, who bolted out into the garden, slamming the kitchen door behind her to avoid the goat's horns. The goat enjoyed a spell of charging at the washing machine, the cupboard doors and the waste bin before re-emerging to seek its fellow trespasser, then it went into the dining-room. It had an enjoyable time charging the sideboard and the drinks cabinet, which revealed yet another goat, and in its eagerness to deal with it shattered precious glasses and bottles of malt whisky before seeing another open door.

This open door was actually the one by which it had entered the house, and so it bolted out and found itself standing in the garden. It rushed onto the lawn just as Tony Harris was returning through the gate. It saw Tony and promptly charged at him. I was later to receive reports of him galloping along the street with the goat in hot pursuit. I think he led the animal back into his own smallholding, but I was then called in. I examined the van, which was still on its side in the driveway of Mr Lynton-Cross's home, and said,

'I'm sorry, Mr Lynton-Cross, but this is not a matter for the police.'

'Why not, for heaven's sake?' he boomed. 'That animal has caused untold damage!'

'The van has overturned on private premises,' I said. 'No other vehicle is involved; it's not on the public road, and so it's not my responsibility.'

'But this damage? To my house, to my collection . . .'

'You'll have to sort that out with Mr Harris' insurance company,' I said. 'If he's comprehensively insured, they will settle matters with you.'

I did establish that Tony had contacted a garage to recover his van, but the case of the bolting goat was not for me, curious and interesting though it was.

I saw Mr Douglas Lynton-Cross several weeks later and asked if he'd obtained compensation for the damage.

'Yes, I did. My collection was not harmed, fortunately, and the insurance company did replace all my damaged furnishings and show cases. It's odd, when Harris came to see me and apologize, he noticed my collection and brought me some of his grandfather's lead soldiers, a sort of apology gift. They were rare ones. I'm pleased to have them, so some good has come of this incident. You know, Mr Rhea, just before that goat incident I was thinking of getting a goat. Someone I spoke to said they brought good luck.'

'It wasn't Tony Harris, was it?' I laughed.

10 'Hello, Young Lovers (Whoever You Are)'

So for the mother's sake, the child was dear.
Samuel Taylor Coleridge (1772–1834)

Surely every family wishes to see its children succeed in life. That success might be in the arts, the sciences, a trade or profession of some kind, a business career or some other vocation or calling. Added to these hopes is romance, for most caring parents also desire their offspring to be happy for ever in love and marriage.

This earnest aim can cause over-keen parents to impose their own ideals upon their children, and the police officer is often in a position to see the ill-effects of this. Fights between a daughter and parents over the former's choice of a boy-friend are common-place, but so are disputes over the son's attempts to woo the girl of his dreams when that girl does not win the approval of his parents.

Wise police officers avoid such conflicts. They regard these traumas as purely domestic and personal and, unless there is some suggestion of law-breaking, they do their utmost to keep a great distance between themselves and the affairs of other people's hearts.

But this is not always possible. Lovesick teenage girls do run away to places like Blackpool or London in search of romance or to get away from unsympathetic parents. In the mid 1960s, moral standards were higher than today, and if these girls were under seventeen, the police would attempt to trace them. The care and protection of juveniles were within our range of duty, and there were two classes of juvenile – anyone under seventeen was called a 'young person', while anyone under fourteen was a 'child' in legal terms. A whole range of offences and crimes could be committed against unprotected juveniles, and the younger they were, the greater the official concern if they ran away from home.

High on the list of our worries were offences against girls. If only because it is an offence for a man to have sexual intercourse with a girl under sixteen, we always sought girls below that age who ran off with 'males', as we termed them (men, youths or boys in ordinary language). If the girl was under thirteen, the penalty for unlawful sex with her was life imprisonment, an indication of society's great concern.

There were several other possible crimes, such as rape, incest, indecent assault, procuring girls for prostitution, abducting them for sex or for their 'estates', as well as cruelty, abandonment, vagrancy and even kidnapping. There were hundreds of evils which might befall a young girl who was tempted away from her home, and so we treated these cases with urgency and compassion.

With this in mind, my head became full of thoughts of horror when I received a telephone call from a Mrs Lavinia Underwood of Newcastle-upon-Tyne.

It was late August, when the moors were quilted with their annual covering of deep purple heather. It was a glorious sight, the rich, aristocratic colouring being enhanced by the greens of the mosses, the blues of the sky and, from time to time, some memorable sunsets.

'Is that the policeman at Aidensfield?' Her voice sounded faint and distant on the line, and I detected a strong Tyneside accent.

'Yes,' I shouted back. 'I'm PC Rhea. How can I help?'

'It's my son,' she said. 'He's been lured away by a young woman.'

'We don't normally get involved in domestic matters.' I interrupted her, wanting to stop her before the story became too involved.

'I know, but I'm so worried. She is not the right sort for him, you see. She's a wrong 'un, Constable. I just wondered if you might trace him and warn him, from me. Find him and tell him to come home, immediately, without her. I don't want him tainted with that hussy.'

'How old is he?' I shouted, for the line was awful. It kept fading and crackling.

'Seventeen,' she said, and upon hearing that troublesome age, I knew I had a problem.

'And the girl?' I called.

'That hussy! She's a good two years younger.'

Now it was a serious matter.

If a girl of fifteen, hussy or not, was missing from home, she had to be found before her experiences gave her adult sensations ahead of her time. I had to know more, and this would mean liaison between our force and Newcastle-upon-Tyne City Police. They might know of the girl's background. I obtained the caller's name and address, but she could not tell me who the girl was. Frank had never said who she was; he'd been very secretive about his romance.

Mrs Underwood described her son as fairly tall, of slim build, with light fair hair and glasses. He had a part-time job in a warehouse, checking the stock. He was wearing a green sports jacket, cavalry twill trousers and brown shoes when he left home, and he'd taken a suitcase of other clothes. He'd left home two days earlier, on the Saturday morning, about 10.30.

'Why do you think he's in this area with her?' I asked.

'He said he was going on a farmhouse holiday near Ashfordly,' she shouted at me. 'He's taken my car, you see. We once stayed there, when he was younger, me and my husband and Frank. He liked the area, he loves the moors, he often goes back, especially when the heather's blooming. And now it's blooming, eh?'

'It is indeed, Mrs Underwood, and it looks wonderful. Now, the car? Can I have a description? Its registration number would be a help.'

She could describe it accurately; it was a Morris Minor, green colour, and she gave me its number. She could not suggest an address for Frank because he'd stayed in different bed-and-breakfast places, ranging from farms to cottages, but all had been in or around Ashfordly to afford him easy access to the moors. He liked walking among the heather in the early autumn, he liked to hear the cry of the grouse and the call of the curlew. He'd be somewhere on those moors, she assured me, with that hussy at his side. I took her phone number so that I could keep in touch, and promised every effort to trace her son. It would not be difficult to check every boarding house or similar establishment.

The truth was, of course, that my determination to find Frank was not for the reasons desired by Mrs Underwood. Her motives might be to save him from an awful marriage – mine were to rescue a very young damsel who might be in official distress. I knew that we had to find the couple to prevent crimes being committed against the girl, even though she might be happy to permit such law-breaking.

After replacing the phone and rubbing my ears to counteract the awful noises the defective line had produced, I rang Newcastle police and asked for the Juvenile Liaison Bureau. A W/PC Collier answered. She listened intently as I explained the situation.

I asked if she had (a) any knowledge of Frank Underwood and (b) any report of a 15-year-old girl's being reported missing from home. She asked me to hang on while she checked her card index. After a few minutes, she said that there was no record of a Frank Underwood in their files – and their files contained the names of all juveniles from that area who might be causing concern, or who might be on the fringes of requiring care or protection, or who had been through the courts. But she would enter his name just in case it cropped up elsewhere.

She did say, however, that six girls were missing from their homes within the city police area, only one of whom was fifteen. She was Margaret Ellison, and W/PC Collier gave me an address in Jesmond, followed by a description of the child. I noted all this down and thanked her, but she did emphasize that Margaret Ellison had been missing for three months. Her parents had received postcards from London and Brighton, saying the girl was all right, but no address had been given. The most recent card had been received only three days earlier, but that still allowed time for Margaret to have met Frank in Ashfordly since Saturday last. It was now Monday.

'It doesn't sound as if he's with Margaret,' she added. 'We have every cause to think she's in the south with a youth called

Gibbons. Taking a country holiday is not her kind of fun. She's not for tramping through the heather with the wind in her hair – she's a city girl, she likes the bright lights, night-clubbing, amusement arcades, fairgrounds and so on.'

'Even so, I'll have to check it out,' I said.

'Keep in touch,' she replied in her strong Tyneside accent, and I rang off.

Next I called Ashfordly police office and spoke to Sergeant Bairstow, explaining the circumstances and saying I now intended to carry out an immediate search of the area. He said he would enter details in our occurrence book so that other officers could also watch out for the little green Morris Minor. It did not escape my attention that, if this couple were staying locally in boarding houses, they would probably give false names and addresses to their hosts, and entries in the guests' registers might also be false. They could be one of the countless Mr and Mrs Smiths who visit such places. But I could try.

It was around 10.30 that Monday morning when I left home in my official van for this tour of the local bed-and-breakfast accommodation. It was not a difficult task to conduct organized visits. We maintained our own lists of these premises simply because so many people asked us for addresses to stay, and so I began my enquiries. I visited each in turn, giving a description of the couple and the car, together with their correct names, emphasizing Frank's name rather than the girl's. But none had a teenaged couple staying with them, and none had entries of a Mr and Mrs Underwood in their registers. I spent the whole of that Monday on that task and failed to locate them.

I knew that my colleagues would do likewise when they came on duty, and so on the Tuesday I checked their visitations to avoid duplication and set off again. By lunchtime I had driven miles and checked eighteen bed-and-breakfast houses, five farms and one private hotel, all without result.

And then, after my packed lunch of cheese sandwiches, fruitcake and coffee from a flask, I crossed the moorland ridge from Lairsdale into Whemmelby. It was there that I saw the little green car. It was parked beside a small plantation of Scots pines and occupied a tiny lay-by where fire-fighting equipment stood in case of emergencies. The registration number confirmed it was the car I sought. I tried the doors; they were locked. Of the couple, there was no sign.

I knew this area well: a footpath ran across the moors at this point, and they could be anywhere along that path, in either direction. If I walked one way, they might have gone the other, and so I decided to wait, at least for an hour or two. I radioed Eltering police office to report my location and decision; they would inform Ashfordly office and Sergeant Bairstow.

And so I sat and waited.

There were some reports I could complete, so my vigil was not wasted. I had several returns, one accident report, a schedule of stock registers and a list of some visits to licensed premises to finalize, so I sat and worked, with the window down and the official radio burbling.

I enjoyed the scent of the heather as it mingled with the strong resin of the pines. I heard skylarks singing high in the heavens somewhere beyond my vision, and the burbling song of the curlew. All around, nature was busy with its own life, and the moorland creatures were preparing for autumn; soon those curlews would head for the coast, the silver birches would lose their leaves but the skylarks would remain to fill the moors with their distinctive song.

As I enjoyed those few hours alone, I saw an elderly couple, a man and woman, heading towards me. They were weaving their way through the high heather, following the sheep track which formed the footpath, and I saw that they were clad in hiking gear. Brightly coloured waterproof leggings and boots, warm kagouls and close-fitting woollen hats completed their outfits, and each carried a small rucksack. Both were using thumbsticks too, and they were moving at a swift pace. They were a couple accustomed to the moors and completely confident on a walk of this kind. I decided to ask if they had seen the teenagers during their rambling.

I waited until they had climbed through the V-shaped stile in the dry-stone wall and then hailed them.

'Excuse me,' I greeted them with a smile, 'I'm looking for a young couple, teenagers, a boy and a girl. I wonder if you've seen anyone during your walk?'

They looked at each other, and in a Tyneside accent the man said, 'Sorry, no. We've not seen a soul, have we, Joyce?'

The woman, in her late sixties, shook her head.

'No, we've been out there all morning, Officer,' she said in that distinctive, lilting accent. 'It's been lovely, mind, not a soul; we've had the whole moor to ourselves. But are they lost or something?'

'Not exactly,' I said, 'but they're from your part of the world.' I referred to their accents. 'The lad's run away and taken the girl with her – she's only fifteen.'

'Oh dear, it happens all the time,' said the woman. 'I used to be a teacher, and you'd be surprised how many fourth-form lasses ran off with sixth-form lads!'

'Are you staying in the area?' I asked.

'Aye,' smiled the man. 'We're at Spout House Farm near Gelderslack, bed-and-breakfast.'

'There's no teenagers there, is there?' I asked hopefully, for I had not yet visited that farm.

'No,' he said. 'Just us. But if we do see them, we'll call you. Ashfordly police, isn't it?'

'That's the nearest police station. We'd be most grateful,' I said. 'Well, thanks anyway.'

As they turned to leave, the man went towards the little green car. He produced a key and opened the door.

'Er, excuse me,' I said, wondering if I was about to make a fool of myself, 'but is that your car?'

'Well, not exactly, Officer. It's my mother's.'

My brain did a very, very rapid mental exercise.

'Is she Mrs Underwood?' I asked very slowly, and I gave her address.

'She is,' said the man.

'And, at the risk of seeming a total fool, are you Frank Underwood?' I was looking at his physical appearance. In spite of his age, he did have strands of fair hair protruding from his hat, and he matched the description of the 'youth' I was seeking.

'I am. You don't mean she's reported me missing? The silly old fool . . .' he laughed. 'Look, what did she say, Constable?'

I did not wish to repeat her description of the lady at his side, so I said she'd called me to say her son had disappeared with a young woman and that she'd given me the impression he was seventeen.

'Seventeen? I'm seventy!' he laughed. 'I'm seventy, officer. I am grown up, you know!'

And now I realized what I'd done. The fault on the line had made me mis-hear that word. I'd thought he was seventeen and had deduced, wrongly, that his girl was fifteen, whereas she was probably sixty-eight. I did not ask!

The couple laughed at my embarrassment. Frank explained how possessive his mother had become since she had been widowed – she was ninety-two now, but remarkably fit. Frank, himself a widower, had for a time lived with his mother, but now he'd met Joyce he had decided to allow himself a bit of romance and freedom. He'd borrowed her car because his own was undergoing a complete service. Amazingly, she was still fit enough to drive and insisted on running her own car.

'I've never told mother where Joyce lives, or who she is or anything about her,' he admitted. 'If that seems selfish, Constable, forgive me, but if I did tell mother, she'd pester the life out of Joyce, trying to get her to end her relationship with me. And so I keep Joyce a secret from mother. She's tried to use you to find out who she is – the crafty old thing!'

'So what are you going to do now?' asked Joyce, smiling in her amusement.

'I'm going to ring Newcastle police Juvenile Liaison Bureau to cancel their records of the 17-year-old Frank Underwood. I'm going to confirm that he has not run away with 15-year-old Margaret Ellison (who is missing from that area) and I'm going to ring Mrs Underwood to say that her son is safe and that his private affairs are nothing to do with the police.'

'You won't say where we are, will you? Or that you've found us?'

'No,' I said. 'I promise.'

We departed on good terms, the couple chuckling at their curious experience, and I returned to Ashfordly to explain this clanger to Sergeant Bairstow. But he took it in good part and said he would cancel the searches going on elsewhere.

He would endorse the record, 'Underwood traced with adult partner. No offences revealed.' That would prevent daft questions from higher authority.

When I returned home, my wife and I laughed at the development, and then the telephone rang. It was Mrs Underwood.

'I'm ringing to see if you have found my son yet,' she said the line still crackling and faint.

'Yes,' I said, without going into details. 'I gave him your message and he thanked me.'

'Well, if you see him again, Officer, tell him I'm not feeling very well. Tell him I've had another of my dizzy turns and I think he should come home – without that hussy of course.'

'Yes, I'll do that, Mrs Underwood,' I said.

To clear myself, I rang Mr and Mrs Jackson, the owners of Spout House Farm at Gelderslack, to ask them to pass on the 'sickness' message to Mr Underwood.

'Underwood?' asked Helen Jackson. 'I'm sorry, Mr Rhea, there's no one called Underwood here. Our only guests at the moment are two pensioners, a Mr and Mrs Smith from Newcastle-on-Tyne.'

A story of comparable mother-love involved Mrs Lucy Haines of Crag Top Farm, Briggsby. A great deal younger than Lavinia Underwood (and much younger even than Lavina's son, Frank), she was the widow of Michael Haines. He was a farmer who had died in his early forties. His sudden and early departure from this life meant that Lucy was left with the farm to run and five sturdy sons to rear. In both challenges, she succeeded admirably, for the farm was well run and profitable, while her sons had all responded to their new responsibilities by working hard on the farm before launching themselves into fresh careers.

As Lucy nudged towards her middle fifties, the eldest four sons had all left home. After their youthful taste of the tough work on the farm, they had decided on easier careers.

Andrew had joined the army, Simon had found work in London, first as a motor mechanic and then as a taxi-driver, Paul was doing well as a quantity surveyor with a building company in the Midlands, while John had opened an electrical goods shop in York. Only Stephen, the youngest, was still at home. Now in his middle twenties, he worked alongside his mother, the pair of them slogging from dawn till dusk to keep the farm viable. It was a busy, non-stop life of hard work, for they had a large dairy herd, pigs, sheep and poultry, as well as many acres of arable land which produced barley, wheat and potatoes. That was what Michael Haines had established before his death – he'd worked so hard to create a profitable farm which he could pass to his sons.

The farm occupied a splendid site. Its buildings formed a kind of defensive cluster around the sturdy, stone-built farm house. In some ways, it was like a castle, because the foldyard was akin to a courtyard, with the buildings arranged around it to form a protection against the bitter weather which could blow across that hill top. The house was like the keep, while the barns and outbuildings formed the battlements. The entire group of buildings stood on the summit of a limestone crag with a winding, unmade road leading down to the dale below. The fields were spread across the lofty plain, and some of the slopes were covered with deciduous trees. I always enjoyed the ride back from Crag Top, if only for the long views one could obtain from the descent.

In his endeavours to carve a working farm from that lonely site, Michael Haines had had some help – an aged farmworker called Ralph had supported him for the whole of his (Michael's) life and most of Ralph's. Ralph had started work here when he was fifteen and had worked for Michael Haines' father. Even though the widowed Lucy was never financially well-off, she would never consider getting rid of Ralph. He was part of the establishment and had, over the years, been largely responsible for creating a working farm around this lofty house. Following Michael's death, however, the bulk of the work fell upon the broad shoulders of Lucy and Stephen, because Ralph was, quite simply, too old to undertake the heavier tasks. The years of toil had taken their toll, and he should really have retired by now. But he did not leave – he stayed on to help and would probably stay there until he dropped dead. Unmarried, he knew no other life and lived in a rented cottage in the village.

Ralph's work was his life – and so it was with Lucy and her son. Neither she nor Stephen went anywhere for social outings or holiday visits – they had never been to any of the other sons' homes, for they never had the time or the money; they never took a day off unless it was to visit a local mart or perhaps the Great Yorkshire Show at Harrogate. For them, their farm was their entire life, even if it was a never-ending routine of near drudgery. Lucy saw no alternative; born of moorland farming stock, her parents had also lived this kind of life.

In spite of living in the middle 1960s, Stephen had found himself emulating his mother's early years. It seemed he was destined to follow his ancestors into a life of hard work and little relaxation. I don't think he'd had a girl-friend since leaving school, and I never saw him pop into the local pub for a drink or join the other lads into the cricket or football teams. He was almost a recluse at the grand old age of twenty-five. The only time I noticed him around the village was when he came down to the garage to purchase spares for the tractor. He spent hours working on the tractor, fixing defects, polishing it, mending broken bits and devising modifications of his own. There were few local lads more keen and knowledgeable about tractors.

I did, of course, see both mother and son during my regular visits to the farm. I had to visit the premises at least once a quarter to check the stock register, and there were other occasions of duty, such as renewal of their firearms and shotgun certificates, or warnings if outbreaks of notifiable diseases of animals were suspected within the county. During my visits, I grew to like Lucy. She was a stocky woman scarcely more than five feet in height and slightly overweight in spite of her hard work. She had a round, ruddy face, very dark and pretty eyes, good white teeth and jet black hair which hinted at Continental or gypsy ancestry, though I don't think she had any foreign blood in her veins, for many moorland girls had these dark good looks.

Her face was weathered and tanned and she usually wore her hair tied back in a bun. Her attire about the farm was generally a heavy frock worn beneath a well-used pinny, with an old cardigan about her shoulders in winter, and black wellingtons on her feet all the year. I had never seen her dressed in smart clothes – even when she visited Ashfordly market on a Friday for her fruit and groceries, she wore that old cardigan and her wellies. But, I often thought, she was a good-looking woman who, with a little care and thought about her appearance, could have attracted a fine man – as indeed she once had.

The villagers, myself included, often wondered why she did not sell the farm to provide herself with an income from the capital it would generate. Oddly enough, she gave me a clue during a visit one September.

I called one misty morning, and Lucy produced a mug of coffee and a scone, asking me to join her, Stephen and old Ralph at the kitchen table. She brushed aside some mountaineering books which were on the table, and then Stephen came in and, blushing slightly, removed them to the sideboard. I wondered if he was taking up a new hobby, for these were colourful books full of photographs and descriptive passages, but I did not embarrass him by asking.

'You look tired,' I said to Lucy as we settled down for a chat over the coffee. Stephen had left us, taking his coffee and Ralph's outside, saying there was work to be done in the foldyard.

'He's very shy,' she said, as if in apology for Stephen's awkwardness in company.

'I know the feeling!' I smiled, knowing that some country lads were painfully shy in company of any kind, especially that of girls. 'But how about you? Are you working too hard?'

'Mebbe I am.' She regarded me with a friendly look. 'It makes me realize I'm getting older, Mr Rhea. I'm past fifty, you know.'

'Well you don't look it.' I hoped I was not being patronizing by merely stating the obvious. 'But you can't go on for ever. You ought to sell up and invest the money, and enjoy the result of all your hard work.'

'There's many times I've thought of doing that.' I thought I detected a note of yearning in her voice. 'But Michael wouldn't have wanted it. He was building up this farm for the lads – that's all he worked for.'

'But they've left the farm.' I wondered if I was being too forward in reminding her of this, but I felt I could be honest.

'Aye,' she sighed. 'That's summat Michael never foresaw. He saw all his sons taking over, sharing the work and expanding the farm. He trained them for that – and then he died. They stuck it for a while, but they'd had enough of long hours and hard work with no money to spend. They've all gone, except our Stephen. Mind, if I go, the farm'll be theirs, to share. They're all part-owners, even if I do all the work.'

'And what about Stephen?' I asked. 'Will he stay?'

'I don't know,' she sighed. 'What I would like, Mr Rhea, is for him to find a good, hard-working and honest lass, one who's been bred on the moors, one who'll take to this kind of life. Then he'd stay, he'd produce some bairns, and the farm could be kept in the family just as Michael wanted, and then handed down. The others say they don't want it; they've said I should sell up, and they'll let me have their shares till I die. But, well, there's Stephen. He needs the work, he'd not find anything else, you know . . .'

As we chatted, I could see that she was actually working for Stephen's benefit but I also knew there was no guarantee he would stay to farm this lonely, hilltop site. She ought to be thinking of herself now, she should retire and enjoy her investment, for the farm would bring a high sum on the open market.

As our conversation continued and I accepted her second mug of coffee, she smiled and asked me a favour.

'I'd like you to do something for me, Mr Rhea.' Those dark eyes scanned my face. 'A favour, if you will.'

'I hope I can.' I was cautious, wondering what was to come.

'You remember when I towed you out of that ditch last winter?' she reminded me.

I remembered the incident. In my police van, I had skidded into a ditch on the outskirts of Aidensfield, and she had halted with the tractor. She'd towed me out; there was no damage to the police van and I had never reported it to anyone. But at the time I'd said, 'Thanks, Mrs Haines, if ever you need a favour, well, you know where to come.' And now she was calling in that favour.

'I remember,' I said. 'And I'm always grateful.'

'Well, now I'm asking a favour in return.'

I wondered what was coming.

'It's our Stephen,' she said quietly. 'He never goes out Mr Rhea, he never goes where he's likely to meet a girl. I wish he'd go to the pub or join something but he spends all day working and won't go out. He thinks of nowt else but tractors, and at night he'll sit in to watch television or read.'

'So how can I help?' I wondered.

'Well, you're out and about all the time, meeting people. I wondered if you knew of any suitable lasses, farm lasses like me, who'd make him a friend. He needs a friend, Mr Rhea, a girl-friend. I thought, well, that if you did know of anybody that might suit him, you'd let me know.'

'I will,' I said. 'Just now, I can't think of anyone, but if I do, I'll get in touch.'

'You won't forget?' I realized she was very serious about this.

'No, I won't forget,' I said, taking my leave.

I never regarded myself as a matchmaker, and furthermore. I knew the dangers that could result from such arrangements, but I did not forget her earnest plea. As I motored around the moors, calling at farms and remote houses, I often recalled Lucy's words, but all the desirable young ladies in those areas were 'spoken for', as we termed it. I never saw anyone I thought would tolerate the harsh life of Crag Top Farm or be strong enough to cope with Stephen's painful shyness.

But then, some eighteen months after that chat with Lucy, I visited Marshlands Hall at Gelderslack at the request of the occupants, a Mr and Mrs Slater. They had come to this old manor house and had turned it into fine private hotel; now, to take advantage of the changes in the licensing laws, they wanted to apply for a table licence which would permit them to sell intoxicants to non-residents who took meals in their dining-room. I went along to discuss this with them, armed with my knowledge of the liquor licensing laws.

Bernard and Olive Slater were practical folks who saw the potential in their idea. As I chattered to them, I noticed a young woman working in the grounds. She was hammering some fence posts into the earth with a huge mallet. The Slaters noticed my interest.

'That's Sylvia,' said Olive Slater. 'Our daughter. She's an outdoor type if ever there was one.'

'Does she work here?' I asked out of interest.

'Sort of,' said her father. 'She spends her time rushing all over the world. Her great-aunt – my aunt Felicity – left her some money, so she is almost independent of us. But she uses this house as her base and earns her keep when she's here by working, sometimes outside like she is now, and sometimes by waiting at table or even decorating. She's a real tomboy and a useful handywoman.'

'She's just come back from a climbing expedition in the Alps,' her mother said. 'And before that, she sailed every lake in the British Isles, and she's trekked to the source of every Yorkshire river . . .'

'She sounds a restless sort of lass!' I laughed.

'She ought to be settling down,' her father joked. 'She's nearly thirty now, and there's no sign of a man in her life. If you know of any young men who could meet her challenge, I'd be grateful – she's always too busy rushing off to meet any local lads.'

At this, I recalled Lucy's plea about her Stephen. Here were two young people, each isolated in their own way, with no hope of meeting one another, and for a fleeting moment I wondered if they had anything in common. As I watched the powerful Sylvia hammering in those fence posts, I thought she might be ideal for Stephen. Where else would a farmer find a girl capable of doing a man's work?

'I might know just the lad,' I said, and told them about Stephen Haines.

'We think she'd do well with a place of her own,' said Olive Slater. 'She needs to settle down and extend some of her energy making it a success – she's got nothing at the moment, you see, except a bit of cash which won't last for ever. She can't go on for ever rushing around the world on her own. This isn't our own premises, we rent it, so we can't pass it on.'

'Well,' I said, 'I'm sure the Haines could use some help from time to time. Whether she and Stephen hit it off remains to be seen.'

'Tell Mrs Haines to give us a call if she does need help about the farm,' invited Bernard Slater, 'and I know our Sylvia will welcome the change – and the bit of cash. If a romance blossoms, well, that's a bonus. We'd rather she became independent instead of using us as a base and, let's face it, a convenience. We do have a permanent staff, and we can't pay any of them off every time our Sylvia decides to come home. We'd never get them back when she left.'

'So something away from here would be an asset?' I said.

'Ideal,' said Bernard Slater. 'I think she could do with some work away from here.'

It was another three months before I revisited Crag Top Farm, and I found Lucy with her arm in plaster. She had fallen off the roof of an outbuilding while replacing some loose tiles and had broken her wrist.

'How are you coping?' I asked. I knew that winter is a quiet time on the farm, but I also knew that much does require attention in winter, especially maintenance work. With one person incapacitated, life would not be easy.

'I'll be honest. I'm not coping,' she said. 'Our Stephen is doing his best, but the cattle take most of his time, and I'm tied to the house now. There's fencing to do, ditching and so on . . . and there's no workers available just now. They won't work for farm wages, and poor old Ralph's getting too slow.'

It was then that I recalled Sylvia Slater and, remembering my earlier conversation with Lucy, I said, 'I know just the person!'

I explained that Sylvia was older than Stephen by a year or two, but that she seemed a capable lass so far as outdoor work was concerned. She might be willing to come along if she wasn't canoeing down the Amazon, hiking through the Grand

Canyon or rebuilding ruined castles. Lucy listened intently and smiled.

'She might be just the sort to jerk our Stephen out of his shyness.'

I gave her the number of Marshlands Hall Hotel before I left.

As I was on holiday at the time of the next quarterly visit to the farm, the stock registers were inspected by a colleague, and so there was a gap of six months before I returned to Crag Top Farm. By then it was summer, and the countryside was looking its best. The hedgerows were in full leaf, buttercups covered the floor of the dale with their golden blooms, and forget-me-nots decorated the woods around Crag Top.

The farm was smart and tidy as I knocked on the kitchen door. It was opened by Stephen, who invited me in as his mother would have. He and old Ralph were having their 'lowance, as the mid-morning break is called, and both were sitting at the scrubbed wooden kitchen table. Blushing slightly, Stephen invited me to join them. He had made some coffee in a pan, and there was a fruitcake on the table. I smiled and accepted.

Stephen produced the necessary books from the bureau without my having to ask and laid them in front of me before joining me over coffee. But of Lucy there was no sign. Ralph said nothing but merely grinned at me as Stephen sat and looked into his coffee mug. Conversation would not be easy. But where *was* Lucy?

'Your mum not around?' I asked eventually.

He shook his head. 'She's gone mountaineering,' he said, then added quickly, 'She allus has had a liking for mountains, and when that lass o' Slater's came to help out, they decided to have a month off. They're gone to Canada, to the Rockies.'

Good for Lucy! I was surprised at this sudden abandonment of the farm, but I smiled at Stephen.

'She's a fine lass, that Sylvia,' I said.

'She's too bossy for me,' he grunted. 'She's as bad as my mother, so I'm off when they get back, Mr Rhea.'

'Off?' I asked. 'Where to?'

'Hull,' he said. 'There's a new tractor distributor opened there. They were advertising for a tractor mechanic. I got the job. I start next week.'

'And the farm? What's going to happen to that?'

'Mum and Sylvia will run it,' he said quietly, getting up to return to his task.